Christian Responsibility in Economic Life

CHRISTIAN PERSPECTIVES
ON SOCIAL PROBLEMS

Gayraud S. Wilmore, *General Editor*

Christian Responsibility in Economic Life

by
ALBERT TERRILL RASMUSSEN

100036
Philadelphia
THE WESTMINSTER PRESS

LIBRARY OF CONGRESS CATALOG CARD No. 65–10209

PUBLISHED BY THE WESTMINSTER PRESS ®
PHILADELPHIA, PENNSYLVANIA

PRINTED IN THE UNITED STATES OF AMERICA

Contents

Foreword

THIS BOOK IS ONE OF SEVERAL TO APPEAR DURING the next few years in a series entitled Christian Perspectives on Social Problems. This is an attempt to meet a challenge from an exceedingly robust minority of laymen for brief, readable analyses of cultural problems from a theological perspective. It is intended to help them *think theologically* about some of the exasperatingly difficult problems of society, both the issues relating to life in America and those linking this nation to the destiny of the world.

Recent researches on family life have found laymen obsessed with "loving, happy relations" in the family, with child-rearing and personal problems of status and adjustment, but with little comprehension of how private troubles bisect public issues. This curious fascination with selfhood to the neglect of neighborhood is not, however, a universal malaise of Protestantism. A minority, perhaps, but a minority that refuses to be lightly regarded by ecclesiastical officialdom, is demanding to know the meaning of events of our day for the Christian faith and to demonstrate the critical and renewing power of faith in secular society.

It is to these doughty men and women that the several volumes of the Christian Perspectives on Social Problems series are directed, and it is hoped that they not only will

1

make for an unsettling reading experience but will provide stimulating material for small-group study and discussion. To that end, questions for discussion are appended to each of the books as starters for fruitful controversy.

Professor Rasmussen, a leading exponent of the "contextual" position in Christian ethics, does not solve the problem of American economic life in this volume. He does not work miracles with antiquated moral absolutes and ideal prescriptions. His purpose is to explain whence we have come, by what routes, and how we have been misled by a business creed that is a secularization of the classical Protestant ethic.

It cannot be doubted that economic irresponsibility is rampant. Americans consume about 35 percent of the world's goods and services with 6 percent of the world's population. Yet one fifth of American families subsist on incomes of $2,000 a year or less. Industry lags behind its productive capacity. Public services and social welfare are shamefully inadequate. The glitter and glamour of World's Fairs and garish entertainments mask the psychological and structural sickness and insecurity of our life and distract us from the real dilemma of businessmen and the masses, who both benefit from our economy and increasingly commit suicide because of it. As Hendrik Kraemer once said, Americans may never have had it so good, nor have they ever been in greater peril.

Professor Rasmussen concludes that the committed self as decision maker and the church as the defining context of decision provide our road signs. Overarching his synthesis of the elements of contemporary economic reality is the sovereignty of God and his claim upon us to be responsible participants in the world as it is and as God brings it to fulfillment.

GAYRAUD S. WILMORE

Pittsburgh, Pennsylvania

Chapter I

The Tragic Separation

IN THE TRAGIC SEPARATION BETWEEN RELIGION AND daily life, no area has developed a wider gap than that between faith and economic affairs. This has happened in spite of the fact that the doctrine of Christian vocation was a key emphasis of the Reformation, and Calvinism has been called the spiritual midwife of capitalism. The result of the split has been to make faith irrelevant and barren and economic life sterile and without higher purpose. The unfortunate result is that men are compelled to live in the hazardous and complicated world of occupational life without the sense of sacred calling, while their religious lives must be lived in ghostly and disembodied detachment from the arena of action and decision.

In fact, this separation has become so accepted that many people, both loyal devotees of Christianity and hardheaded devotees of business enterprise, will be horrified at the very suggestion that there has been or can be an intimate and significant relationship between the two. So compartmentalized have the various concerns of human endeavor become in our time that even those people who are at the same time religiously active and business-oriented often embrace this split within themselves.

It is the purpose of this short book to attempt to bridge

3

this gap and recover the historical connection in our tradition. We believe the gap has been due to several radical misunderstandings of both the classical Biblical Protestant faith and the processes of economic activity.

Fortunately, there are clear indications that many theologians and moralists have climbed down from their ivory towers to take a fresh theological look at the real world and that men of affairs are hopefully seeking new illumination and guidance from the great traditions that have shaped our history and made us what we are.

A lively new interest is being displayed in our leading schools of business administration and in many journals of business and economic affairs in a search for ethical guidelines for economic responsibility. Chief Justice Earl Warren, in an address reported on the front page of *The New York Times,* called for a new profession of ethical counselors, similar to legal counselors, as consultants to business organizations. There has been appearing a whole spate of books on business ethics, including one by Luther Hodges, the Secretary of Commerce of the United States (*The Business Conscience;* Prentice-Hall, Inc., 1963).

Unfortunately, many of these discussions still reveal a continuation of some of the misunderstandings that created the separation in the first place. Some of these misunderstandings are on the religious and ethical side and take the form of a few legalistic generalizations that are believed to exhaust the religious contribution to economic activity. Others are misunderstandings or oversimplifications concerning economic organization and the character of the actual processes of decision-making in the economic sphere.

Therefore the time seems ripe for a creative discussion between economic theorists and practitioners and the interpreters of our Christian faith. This essay is a modest attempt to join the brisk discussion already under way.

We shall attempt to look realistically at the radical changes that are calling into question many of our old moral assurances and many of our trusted patterns of action. We shall look at the historical trends and misunderstandings that have created the gap between theological and economic interpretations. Finally, we shall ask, How does the Christian participate faithfully and creatively in the economic process?

THE SPIRITUAL AND ETHICAL SIGNIFICANCE OF ECONOMIC LIFE

Several false or oversimplified distinctions have created the gap between Christian ethics and economic action. The first is the popular division between the spiritual and the material under which faith is presumed to deal with the spiritual and economic activity with the material. This has also been called the conflict between faith and facts or between ideals and hard economic realities. However, whether recognized or not, occupational life has central spiritual significance for human beings; and, conversely, spiritual life has an inevitable and dominating effect upon economic life. By spiritual life, a highly misleading term that we use very gingerly, we mean the rich inner life of cherished values, meanings, and loyalties that comprise the mysterious central identification of selfhood, as well as the value content of whole cultures. These are the distinguishing attributes of persons as contrasted to things. The spiritual life, it must be noted, is not "the good" aspect of man; it is simply the core of selfhood that is the seat of both his corruption and his creativeness. Religious faith is the ultimate devotion or the supreme relationship under which selfhood is centered and sustained.

The notion of a separation between the spiritual and the material, or between worship and occupation, is clearly foreign to the Biblical perspective. The Israelites looked upon all aspects of life under the vivid consciousness of living in a covenant community under a sovereign God who ruled over all things. They lived in a sacramental world and in a theocratic society in which a compartmentalization of familial, political, economic, and religious life was unknown. All were part of God's creation. To the Old Testament prophets, economic exploitation and injustice were a direct affront and an act of unfaithfulness to their God.

Prof. George Ernest Wright and a distinguished panel of scholars in their World Council Biblical Studies Book (*The Biblical Doctrine of Man in Society;* SCM Press, Ltd., London, 1954) find the same integrated world view in the New Testament as in the Old. In Christ a new covenant is established with the whole people of God.

Economic life was not separated out and dealt with as a special sphere, because it was all an integral part of life in God's world lived in relation to him. Occupational pursuits were not looked upon as evil or inferior. Material abundance was considered a blessing from God, and the right to hold property was assumed. Faithful stewardship was expected, and many sharp warnings were issued by Jesus concerning the misuse of wealth and its corrupting possibilities. An inordinate interest in its acquisition could usurp dependence upon and obedience to the Lord. Material wealth was evil only when gained through the impoverishment of the neighbor or when it became an idolatry. Property was held under a higher stewardship to God, and therefore all human ownership was conditional. The Biblical view confirms the characterization of Christianity as the world's most materialistic religion.

The Biblical view may be summarized as one of unity and interdependence between the occupational and religious life. The foundations of the doctrine of Christian vocation are found in the teachings of Jesus and the writings of Paul, later to be developed by Luther and Calvin.

With this framework in mind, let us turn to some of the specific reasons why occupational life is spiritually and morally of crucial human significance.

First, man is a physical creature who must subsist as an organism before he can exist as a man. He is dependent on the production of food, raiment, and shelter from the resources of nature. This is the foundation of individual life as well as the whole pyramid of human culture and is the base of all higher attainments. Not until a society reaches a level of production that rises above the stark necessities of subsistence can it release many, if any, of its members from enslavement to sheer material necessity. The problem of scarcity and the consequent elemental ethical issue of how to distribute goods in short supply fairly has been the central and probably the originating consideration of economics.

In most societies, until the modern period, the vast majority of men were compelled to live close to the margin of spending all their time and energy for sheer subsistence. Only the very few, because of political dominance or hereditary rights to accumulated property, lived in comparative luxury and affluence. Therefore, only the few had either the time or means to engage in activities of discovery or creation.

Secondly, the sustaining culture of values, life-styles, and meanings, which cradles and shapes the consciousness and aspirations into which individuals are nurtured, is profoundly shaped by the economic organization and the ways people make their livelihood. The Marxists have carried this recognition to one-sided extremes, and many Americans of capitalist orientation equal or surpass them in granting supremacy of influence to material production over values systems and sacred devotions. Nevertheless, the shaping power of economic organization and occupational life on all other aspects of existence cannot be denied. It is also important to recognize that this is a two-way circuit in which the goals we cherish and the sacred values we love also influence our work-styles and organizational forms. Man cannot keep his values out of his work or his work out of his values.

In many respects, we live today in a business culture in which commercial values dominate our ethos (the spirit of our times) and all aspects of our society. This has created one of the great paradoxes of American life. As levels of production reach heights that should liberate large blocks of time and resources for spiritual and cultural enrichment, the sheer momentum of the industrial machine threatens to commit us to an even more slavish preoccupation with material production. We may be compelled to buy more and more of what we need less and less in order to maintain the levels of affluence that will leave us no margins for spiritual endeavors.

Mass communications, entertainment, and leisure-time activities are, increasingly, commercially operated and oriented and are becoming compelling commodities. Education seems to be geared more to occupational preparation than to an induction into the appreciation of, and creative participation in, the rich ongoing cultural heritage.

Thirdly, occupation is, increasingly, the primary role-identification that shapes personality and regulates human behavior. The crucial question that is asked of a stranger to identify him in order to guide one's response to him concerns his occupation. In a mass urban society, where neighborhood life and intermediary groupings are disappearing or losing significance, the occupational role becomes the one dependable anchorage of ego-maintenance and self-identity. Furthermore, occupation is compulsory because it is the means of livelihood and loses the optional character of most other roles. Under increasing vocational specialization and employers' demands for prior experience, it is harder to change occupations; and large numbers of people feel trapped and frustrated in their work.

Most human beings spend their largest block of time in their waking hours on the job, meeting its routines and adjusting to its requirements. Even with shorter hours, the job is the orienting preoccupation of life that is difficult to escape. The trend in professional and administrative occupations is for the work load to require longer hours and carry over into leisure time so there is little reprieve from conscious concentration. When one role becomes so central, it may swallow up selfhood and provide no perspective of detachment or self-criticism. A great deal of contemporary literature has focused upon occupational role-enslavement by which persons become almost selfless functionaries or cogs in organizational machines. When occupation usurps the total reason for existence and success in fulfilling it becomes the overriding goal, it becomes destructive. Such work-enslaved people die when they retire, or are wiped out if they lose their positions. Furthermore, they are more vulnerable to unethical shortcuts and success-at-any-price because they have invested worship of the ultimate in occupational position.

In the contemporary world, the vocational function such as engineer, steam fitter, baker, has tended to fuse into the organizational role in a particular corporation. Thus adjustment and position in a particular enterprise shapes the self. In one set of survey interviews, more than half the respondents, in reply to the question concerning occupation, answered, "General Motors" or "Chevrolet," rather than engineer, salesman, or production worker.

Fourthly, economic life is perhaps universally the area of greatest temptation for man. By this we mean that it is the area in which man's inordinate self-assertiveness can be expressed and the opportunity for the exploitation of other human beings, as things, is most afforded. In the impersonal life of buying and selling in an urbanized society in which business transactions take place largely among people who have no other relationship, the restraints of disapproval and the incentives of developing permanent relationships are greatly reduced. People who deal routinely with strangers and with other people's merchandise or money, day after day, are subjected to heavy pressures and few restraints. This is especially true when the owners are remote and rich corporations, or when wealth appears only on paper as bookkeeping entries. In a commercial society where money is status and prestige, where its advantages are paraded daily, and the shops are stocked with novel gadgetry, the temptation secretly to divert or garner a little of it at any price becomes intense.

The requirements of honesty in the intimate relations of family and friends are usually clear and recognized. But, in the complex world of abstract property and slick new ways of selling the intangibles of inside knowledge and operational know-how, moral definitions have often fallen into great confusion. This is why the incidence of petty, and not so petty, ways of "nest-feathering" has become so high. From top executives to supermarket checkers, there is a widespread admission that everybody takes advantageous shortcuts if he feels sure he can "get away with it." If these shortcuts are new and undefined morally or legally and the supreme values honored in our society are monetary, it is not surprising that we confront a serious crisis in trust.

Moreover, when men work in large organizations that develop corporate policies with institutional moral support, personal responsibility loses its sharpness and is diffused across the group. This was the theme of Reinhold Niebuhr's *Moral Man and Immoral Society* (Charles Scribner's Sons, 1932). Doubtful or even corrupt practices, when institutionalized and conventionalized, receive a subtle kind of unquestioned legitimacy. When "everybody" does it and it becomes standard operating procedure, few people raise questions or resist.

Persons who are scrupulously honest in personal affairs and take moral pride in their fidelity to their enterprise may easily take satisfaction in pressing corporate advantage beyond fairness, without the slightest recognition of any blame. Therefore, in addition to providing the exposure to direct temptation to take undue advantage for self, the economic area subjects human beings to the more subtle vulnerability of obscure organizational temptation. Directly pertinent is the well-known recognition that even professional organizations, created to improve efficiency and protect the public, have an almost inevitable tendency to moralize the undue advantage that their cooperative power makes possible. There can be little doubt that moral sensitivity and integrity are tested and threatened in the economic sphere, as in no other, and so often in subtle and obscure forms.

Fifthly, the economic sphere has become the primary context in which human beings must find personal worth and make a contribution that provides a sense of purpose and mission in the world. A sense of uselessness is probably the most debilitating and paralyzing thing that can happen to the human person. To find a significant and important function among one's fellows, in some cause that transcends the self, is imperative for self-conscious and interdependent man. One of the traditional psychological foundations of laissez-faire economic theory was that human nature is inert and lazy and that man has to be goaded to effort by fear of impoverishment or the lure of material incentives. Personal material gain has been given top, if not sole, priority as incentive to action. This view places little faith in the motivations of service or mission. However, this is now open to serious doubt. The

Christian interpretation, although recognizing the necessity of self-maintenance and the inevitable self-centeredness of man, also believes that selfhood withers and is destroyed without a self-transcending calling or purpose. The introverted life, turned in upon itself, for a creature whose very being is relational, spells decline and death.

The Christian sense of vocation adds a dimension to occupation that lifts it above the grind of earning a living and transforms it into a purpose for existence. The economic context, instead of being a battlefield for the struggle for grim survival, becomes the arena of creative expression. Many people without benefit of Christian insight or sense of calling have been able to convert occupation into a satisfying and creative purpose. They still, however, suffer the limitation of depending wholly on the internal pride of successful achievement for its satisfaction. It is doubtful that any Christian entirely escapes the ambiguous character of pride in work well done. However, he also recognizes his inescapable dependence on the efforts of others for his own successes and the fact that their rewards and opportunities are to some degree reduced by his own good fortunes. Self-styled, self-made men are always created and sustained by men and forces far beyond their knowing.

The truly unique factor in Christian vocation is the conviction that the material world with all its resources is God's world and that man's own modest achievements are in no sense his own, but part of a greater history. Most significant of all, the economic arena is a field of divine encounter where every decision is one of accountability to Him. The divine claims are laid upon man not in abstract disengagement but in response to the needs and the claims of all other human actors involved. Therefore, occupation is transformed into vocation; vocation is work done worshipfully, and worship is done vocationally in reference to the transcending relationship to God.

One of the most tragic aspects of the contemporary scene is that many prevailing conditions and values are throwing genuine vocation into jeopardy. Mission, or higher calling through work, is in danger of becoming a modern casualty. Americans were once inspired and motivated by what was called the "gospel of work." This was a highly secularized and inverted version of the Reformation doctrine of Christian calling. Nevertheless, it provided a high-intensity purpose that often extroverted human striving.

The fragmentation of production into minute specializations and separate processes, where no person sees a task carried through to completion, has reduced much work to a meaningless routine. The typical example has been the assembly line, which automation is now making at least partially obsolete. However, at many other levels, even including the functions of many professional men and managers, complex bureaucratic organization assigns such partial responsibility that no one quite understands the total process or recognizes the many results.

This is why a number of studies and summaries have reported that large percentages of men at all levels "hate their work" because they find it unsatisfying and boring. Alexander R. Heron, in his book *Why Men Work* (Stanford University Press, 1943), carefully analyzed war-production data and came to the conclusion that even under the patriotic pressures of wartime, workers showed a high degree of absenteeism, waste, and inefficiency. He concluded that many men who do their best do not work for wage incentives but for some form of mission. Nevertheless, the generalization is often made that we have moved from an economy of production to an economy of consumption. Psychologically, this means that the traditional gospel of work—work for the excitement of creating—is dead; and work for what money will buy has displaced it.

The Personal Versus the Organizational

The second reason for the split between the religious life and the economic life revolves around the distinction between the personal and the organizational. It is assumed that Christian ethics deals with personal relations and inner psychological qualities, whereas economic life operates through external organizations and processes that have their own peculiar dynamics and laws. We have long been confronted with the paradoxical fact that American thinking has been radically system-oriented in economic analysis and person-oriented in the understanding of morality. Our economic system is often eulogized as the most perfect and the most productive system ever devised. Therefore, whenever our economic processes miscarry toward overproduction, toward high unemployment, or regional or class inequities or impoverishments, it is usually considered the fault of immoral or incompetent individuals. (Incompetency is regarded as a vice—"Throw the rascals out and put the good men in, and all the problems will be solved.")

Here again we have a false separation because both sides are highly important and affect each other in reciprocal ways. This is because human persons are not impervious isolates but live their whole lives under institutional forms that condition their attitudes and frame their responsibilities. And, conversely, organizations are formed and administered by individual persons whose qualities and decisions affect their policies and functions. Yet many of the most serious ethical dilemmas involved in economic responsibility arise between the two poles of personal responsibility and organizational limitations; between persons and systems. This is another of the significant gaps that must be bridged. With an increasing majority of people working within corporations and other large-scale organizations created by the "organizational revolution," ethical occupational responsibility must be confronted from both the personal and organizational sides, and it must be frankly recognized that these are not identical.

Most Protestant thinking on occupational life has tended to center around the Reformation doctrine of Christian vocation, which was a central motif for both Luther and Calvin. In the corollary doctrine of "the priesthood of all believers," the Christian was seen as called out of the monastery to serve God in the daily round of producing food and raiment and serving both the physical and spiritual needs of the neighbor. Luther called this "being a Christ to the neighbor" by serving him through participation in the basic productive pursuits of society.

It has sometimes been said that this emphasis on vocation is highly personalized and does not apply to the new organizational world. But a realistic interpretation moves immediately out into the actual arena. It is not simply concerned with an etiquette of politeness on the job, but is interested in the basic structures and patterns that control, limit, or thwart the creative and efficient discharge of responsibility.

Organizations are extremely important in controlling and directing human behavior. Ethical insights and responsible action have to be made "flesh" and structured into organizational patterns just as the "word" had to become flesh in God's revelation of himself in the world. The strict personal approach depends on the long-suffering attitude under which one is supposed to be as decent and honest as bad situations will allow: be friendly and smiling to the gruff and cantankerous, scrupulously honest in a larger situation of organized fraud, hardworking in a context of lethargy and inefficiency.

This type of ethical emphasis deals only with the inconsequential and has little to do with the basic decision-making in regard to efficiency in production, accurate representation of goods and services, fair methods of competition and pricing, or any of the major issues of business. Driven to its logical conclusion, this would mean that slavery could be a Christian economic arrangement if the slaveholders were all good Christians; or that a communist dictatorship would be economically and ethically satisfactory under a benevolent dictator. Few people really believe that putting good people into bad situations produces good moral results.

The Calvinist-Puritan tradition, in particular, recognized the importance of combining both personal and organizational responsibility. In this combined view, it is recognized that not even the best men can avoid unethical practices under oppressive institutional forms, and inversely, under the most balanced and democratically accountable organizations, men who are irresponsible can pervert their functions.

Because of the requirements of technological advance and mass production, our whole society has been moving toward greater organizational coordination and interdependence. Robinson Crusoe or the hermit in the wilderness could subsist by his own efforts, but modern man is dependent upon the coordinated efforts of millions of people he will never see or know. Less than 10 percent of the people in the United States raise all the food. Fifteen thousand pilots and navigators keep the airlines flying. Failure of a small group or a single organization at one point in the process can paralyze our economy. The irresponsibility of a few or the malfunctioning of a single organization, once an irritating problem, can now become a national calamity. This is the hidden vulnerability of our new world.

This whole organizational revolution, to be described more fully in a later chapter, has shifted the basic decision-making process that creates policy in our economy from the personal to the organizational side. Group and corporate decisions are necessarily compromise decisions that must reconcile the judgments of many participants and further the interests of the whole organization. No individual can exercise independent judgment unreconciled in the group process, even when it involves what he regards as important ethical considerations, without resigning. Resigning would simply hand the reconciling task over to someone else willing to make greater concessions. This is why the obstinate moralist finds it extremely difficult to participate in organizational decision-making where responsibility cannot be exercised in a sharply personal manner.

Of course this does not mean that personal leadership and ethical sensitivity are impotent or insignificant, but it does mean that he who is willing to compromise and reconcile differences and settle for actual alternatives is far more likely to achieve more ethical solutions. This is the great paradox of organizational ethics. What the moralist would call "the sin of stooping to conquer" can also be the virtue of reconciling the highest possibility.

The limitations imposed by organizational decision-making are not all on the side of ethical defeat but may also create ethical gains. This is because individuals inevitably have their own biases and moral eccentricities that need to be softened and corrected in interaction with the judgments of others. In large corporations, where policy has far-reaching consequences for the whole society, we can probably be thankful that few are any longer dominated by the long hand of powerful individualists. When important policy decisions must run the gauntlet of approval of executive staffs and boards and face the glare of public opinion, they may be less likely to be one-sided.

On the other hand, there are great dangers in organizational policy-making that defines responsibility and provides group support for the moral justification of its procedures. The lines of accountability may become obscure, ethical considerations seem impersonal and remote, and the advantages of the organization overriding. It may well be that the counterbalancing pressures and restraints are not adequately balanced and the lines of accountability have become obscure in our changing times.

THE CONTENT VERSUS THE CONTEXT

The third form the split between religious and economic life has taken has involved the supposed radical distinction between *the content of faith* and *the context of economic activity*. Under this dichotomy, faith is viewed as content-centered, consisting of abstract beliefs and rigid moral commandments revealed to man by God through literal Biblical teaching or the precepts spoken or exemplified by Jesus. Christian ethics then is a set of fixed rules to be strictly applied to all conceivable situations, including the sphere of economic decisions. Christian responsibility is then regarded as knowing these true ethical principles and building up the courage and self-discipline to apply them rigorously without regard to the unique factors in the situation or the consequences. Knowing the factors involved and the actual alternatives available is considered to be either of secondary importance or ethically irrelevant. Adjustment to what the situation requires or making the best of a difficult dilemma is then thought to be unchristian compromise or immoral expediency.

To men deep in the hurly-burly of business life and working in the decisional arena on the context side, this abstract idealism seems ivory-towered and almost pointless. For those bargaining and dealing in the midst of many limitations, pressures, and claims, the ethical counsel that demands absolute justice or totally self-sacrificing love appears as plain foolishness or carping criticism for daring to participate in the indispensable activities of business at all.

To content-centered moralists and perfectionists, the whole occupational world easily seems to be intrinsically corrupt and sinful and an arena of compromise and unfaithfulness. This whole *Christian-content-versus-worldly-context* way of thinking is bad theology and foolish economics. It is bad theology in contradiction to classical Protestant thinking because it places faith on the side of legalism and moralism and eliminates God's action from the side of economic process. It is foolish economics because it attempts to isolate economic activity from the values and sacred loyalties that are crucial ingredients in all human activity.

We still live under the shadow of an economic tradition that attempted to treat economic behavior as inside a closed system unaffected by other motivations and activities. Economic systems were separated from social, political, and religious systems. The occupational aspect of human personality, labeled "economic man," was isolated from "the spiritual man," "the rational man," "the sexual man," etc., as though the human self could be dissected into unrelated parts. This carving up of both the organizational context of the world and the human personality is false to reality and has created vast mischief in contributing to the gulf between spiritual and occupational life.

The followers of Freud (at least some of them) have argued that human behavior is primarily determined by sexual drives. The cultural determinists have argued that the inner life of man is the product of the values and life-styles of the culture in which they grew up. The Marxists are usually cited as conspicuous examples of economic determinism because they believe that the economic means of production and the modes of property-holding are formative of both man's inner attitudes and all other institutional forms. This relegates the spiritual side of life to the wholly derivative or illusory.

However, Marxists have by no means monopolized the externalized view of man as a product of outside forces. Many capitalist adherents have come perilously close to an equally materialistic view of human existence. They have elevated free enterprise as a system, and material goals as an end, to the position of ultimate value to whose regal demands all else must be adjusted and sacrificed. Man becomes a cog in service to the productive machine rather than its beneficiary.

The most dangerous aspect of this view is that it makes economic responsibility an automatic mechanism built into the impersonal process that is controlled by economic laws. The emphasis on the "hidden hand" of Adam Smith is allowed to obscure the fact that this intricate system could operate in an orderly way only if the great majority of its participants were rigorously self-restrained by deep "moral sentiments" and followed the rules of the game. Nevertheless, many of the doctrinaire classical interpreters have held that noneconomic ethical appraisals and motivations are not only unnecessary and irrelevant, but are external monkey wrenches that jam the smooth-running, self-regulating mechanism, and disrupt the flow of goods and services.

The only part that religion could play was to assure those who still adhered to a faith in Providence that a remote God had enacted this wondrous mechanism and ordained it into an eternal absolute. The economic system itself became the object of worship and man's ultimate trust and fidelity.

What, then, is the religious factor in the Biblical-Reformation tradition if it is neither the content of a legalistic moral code nor the external context of a system

of economic laws created by God to which man must con-
form? How, then, does the Christian find guidance and
motivation as he engages in economic decision-making if
he is deprived of both the moralistic and the mechanistic
solutions?

The Christian answer is far more dynamic and creative
but has no less claim upon our lives than either the
spiritual legalists or the natural-law legalists have supposed. The God of the Christian is one who reveals himself
in acts. He acted in a mighty act of redemption in Christ,
who is the charter, the constitution, and the clue to his
deeds of mercy and reconciliation. He is also acting in
every event into which we move and make our decisions
in encounter and relationship to him. He has called men
through Christ to be active respondents to what he is doing
in the dynamic context of daily life.

Men are redeemed and renewed not apart from their
tasks and decisions but in connection with them and in
the midst of them. They are not redeemed as a reward
for good deeds done or responsibilities enacted but, rather,
gain the insight and courage to be responsive and to act
vigorously as a result of God's initiating and transforming
acts. The place where this God is to be encountered is not
in retreat to a defensive sanctuary but on the job. The time
is not in the remote past or in some new and improved
future, but in the decisive, eternal "now." And the church,
which is the body and vehicle of this living and acting
Lord, is not a separated place or enclosure, but a community of faith, a covenant people, shouldering together
the world's burdens and doing its work as a sacred calling.
This is the Biblical relationship of the content of faith
to the context of action, restored in the Reformation
and most vividly developed in the Calvinist-Puritan tradition. In short, the Christian content is one of acts, not
rules; the worldly context is an arena of interaction with

God and with neighbors who also exist in relationship to him.

The genuine convergence of faith and action, of Christian guidance and economic responsibility, is found in the concrete decision. This is where the inner resources of the Christian's conscience and the external possibilities, framed by the web of situational factors, intersect. The Christian ethic, then, as Joseph Fletcher has put it, "is one of decisions not conclusions." The life it calls for is one of active "holy worldliness."

Chapter II

The Big Change

WE HAVE BEEN PASSING THROUGH A MANY-SIDED revolution that has shifted almost every aspect of the world in which we live. Human beings all live by habits, memories, and tried-and-tested principles; therefore, radical change is disorienting and confusing. Large numbers of people today, like the fictional spaceman who mistakenly went home to the wrong planet, are trying desperately to live in the wrong world—one that no longer exists.

In the midst of swift change, human beings tend to seek security in permanent ideas or rigid moral principles to provide stability and direction. Unfortunately, the big change of this period is total change under which not only physical conditions but value systems, the conventional models and iron laws of economic life, and even sacred religious orientations, are all subjected to serious doubt, as they seem irrelevant and unworkable.

In many ways, the guiding virtues and moral assurances of the free-enterprise man no longer hold, and the iron laws and automatic regulators of the system no longer perform as they once did. This has happened because we have outrun the original situation to which they were fitted. We have learned that economic laws are not eternal

23

truths; they are only theoretical constructions, and are effective only when applicable to ideal conditions. And the ideal conditions necessary are in many ways receding farther and farther from reality. These were: rigorous competition among many producers and automatic balancing between production and buying power.

Similarly time-honored moral laws that have prescribed responsibility are historically relative and were generated in particular contexts. They are not eternal absolutes by which lost security can be recovered in rapid change. Christian commitment can restore validity only in relationship to new kinds of decision and responsibility in the strange, new world.

Perhaps the most profound shock to the religiously faithful has come when they have discovered that some of the presumed moral absolutes of the Christian faith no longer guide conduct into creative channels. For here a basic misunderstanding of the Christian faith is exposed. The unchanging is not to be found in changeless abstractions to be laid down on the dynamics of history, but in the living God himself revealed in Christ. He is the only absolute and unchanging ultimate to whom man owes unconditional allegiance. No age can move beyond his present presence. And this allegiance cannot be expressed by defending old orders or dissolving systems, but only in new acts of responsiveness to God in relevance to new contexts of decision.

THE RADICAL CRISIS IN RAPID CHANGE

One of the great debates of our transitional times concerns whether or not we are undergoing a radical crisis. Americans have been so accustomed to equating sheer change with inevitable progress that rapid change, itself, is welcomed as unquestioned good tidings. Yet a strange paradox appears. When we list our glorious achievements, there is something ominous and threatening to be posted over against every single one:

1. Productive capacity and wealth as measured in GNP (Gross National Product) is the highest in history, yet there still seems to be a heavy sense of anxiety and fear in the business community.

2. The standard of living is soaring to new heights, and more and more people join the expanding middle class that can afford the new benefits of technology. Yet we have become, in many respects, an impoverished, anxious, and neurotic people.

3. Employment is high (although we cannot overlook the millions of unemployed whose lot is particularly demoralizing in the midst of plenty) and majorities have been upgrading their income, yet large numbers in all classes hate or find little satisfaction in their work. There seems to be a more widespread status anxiety and sense of frustration and failure.

4. More people are living in families than ever before, but family breakup and tragic marital conflict is increasing under the hammer pressures of an industrial urbanized civilization.

5. Life expectancy is longer, under vastly improved health services, yet more and more of our aged live longer to endure lonely and disturbed lives.

6. To increasing numbers, there is more leisure time available to cultivate knowledge, personal growth, and richer human relationships; but much of it is wasted in jading distractions and artificial stimulations.

7. The technological breakthrough into the atomic age opens up unbelievable ranges of energy to substitute for grueling hand power, but so far it has been turned largely into instruments for human annihilation.

8. We are devoting more and more of our time and resources to attaining higher educational levels, but there seems to be little enthusiasm for genuine learning and

discovery. Education seems to be increasingly geared to job preparation, under a glorified trade-school orientation.

9. Miracles of mass communication have been achieved, with instantaneous news that opens a wide window onto the whole world, but it has become largely a cheap medicine show, filled with what one social scientist calls "kitsch" (trash).

It is irresponsible not to ask whether this paradox of change is progress or retrogression. The answer of Christians is that change itself is strictly ambiguous; it is neither an impersonal hero nor an inevitable villain. It is the Christian view that God's hand is in every event and turn of history. But this does not absolve men from responsibility to participate in its decisions or guarantee that God will save them from the consequences of their many blunders and insensitivities. Every new achievement has possibilities of destruction or benefit.

The one thing that must be rejected by those who stand in the basic Christian perspective is the notion that social change carries with it an automatic moral progress so that human beings become more sensitive and responsible simply by virtue of gaining greater technical knowledge. Knowledge, or the mastery of facts, is as ambiguous as social change. Every new person who enters the world has to acquire his own commitments and learn his own hard lessons. And every new generation has to reshape its own ethos and modes of responsibility in relation to new kinds of decision.

WHAT IS CRISIS?

The chief reason why radical social change creates a crisis is that it makes obsolete those trusted solutions and patterns by which people have lived in old situations. This is partly because the situations which are faced are no longer definable in the standard categories and thought patterns through which human perception and recognition take place. When we look for the wrong things, there is distortion in what we see and error in our interpretation. The crisis is also created because the originating and sustaining conditions in which the patterns of action were developed no longer prevail.

Another way to put it is that the value systems and the organizational structures no longer mesh. The values and virtues that people have come to love and cherish no longer bear direct relationship to the organizations in which they work and the crucial decisions that they have to make. Strict moralists can bemoan the sad state of irresponsibility and call for vigorous conformity to the old rules of fairness and honesty and yet be wholly irrelevant to the most pressing issues.

On the other hand, in a time of radical flux, the standard value systems themselves may become the casualties. We must be as careful to dissociate ourselves from traditional value systems as we are from giving finality to organizations and their methods. What Emile Dirkheim called a state of "anomie," or normlessness, may prevail under which there is such a diversity and conflict of definitions concerning ethical action that inner confusion reigns. Many men of genuine integrity prefer to be at sea, with no guiding loyalties or values, rather than to fall into the hypocrisy of vigorously defending mores that no longer fit or carry convincing relevancy. If the former type are moralistic defenders of the obsolete, the latter are wishful drifters, adjusting to whatever occurs without a centering identity. Christians ought to escape either pure defensiveness or uncritical drifting.

The big change has created a whole new order of economic life and in a real sense has also created a new order of religious life. Since religious life also exists in the context of society and culture, even though it points to a transcendent reference, it, too, is conditioned by the transition. Religious institutions are interactive respondents being shaped and shaping. Both religious organizations and economic organizations are part of the multiple chain reactions of change. Although it is impossible in brief compass to do more than select a few of the strands of this change as they affect our two chief dimensions of consideration, religious faith and economic activity, let us turn to several interlocking trends.

FROM FOLK SOCIETY TO MASS SOCIETY

In the early stages of American life, the majority of our people lived in small villages or on isolated farms thinly spread across the expanding countryside. This was still true only one hundred years ago, at the time of the Civil War. In a folk society, human beings live in intimate identification and association in local communities and neighborhoods. Their lives and activities were not compartmentalized; religion, occupation, and community overlapped and were common concerns. The sacred was not confined to the church or its internal activities but applied to the planting and harvesting of crops, to concern for neighbors who encountered misfortune, to mutual trust and honor in economic transactions. In a genuine folk society, the people live a sacramental life and there are no strict lines of demarcation between economic life, religious life, and community life.

We must avoid being romantic about American backgrounds and recognize that the intimate folk society was only partial and had its rifts and its deviants. But even though majorities often did not belong to the churches in formal membership, or attend worship, the sacred character of the semifolk society and its common overlap prevailed in the consciousness of most of the people.

Today the dissolution of the folk society is virtually complete except in isolated hamlets, and even here many of the forces of urbanization have penetrated. Only in a few highly resistant religious communities, such as among the Amish and Mennonites, has the change been avoided.

In the metropolitanized society, into which we have been swiftly moving, several new characteristics prevail. There is a fragmentation of organizational life in which separate institutions with separate personnel serve each separate type of human need or concern. Part of this is due to the highly proliferated division of labor. One vocational directory shows over eighteen thousand separate types of occupation. Health services, educational services, religious services, recreational functions, specialized retail sales, etc., are all provided by separate agencies or businesses. Education is what happens in school, religion is an activity that happens in church, business is what transpires at the office or store; and there is little overlap in the people who associate, in the conversational concerns and in the intimacy of relationships. Compartmentalization of function becomes a compartmentalization of concern.

The sheer proliferation of function and the compartmentalization of interests, created by the new type of social organization, is probably a significant causal factor in the separation of occupational life from religion. They simply operate in different contexts. In a highly secular society, more people may go to church and yet display little concern with its basic purposes and commitments; just as in an earlier folk society, fewer people went to church but may have had a more intense religious consciousness. In a mass society, religious faith becomes a private concern severed from the practical preoccupations that absorb most of the time and interest of even the most religiously active laymen. When a religion is no longer the focal identification of selfhood, it is no longer a true religion. It has been displaced by whatever is the new supreme devotion. When Christians come to the point where occupation is the overriding identification and faith is a secondary psychological support, they have, whether recognized or not, changed gods and have abandoned historic Christianity.

The second result of the urbanized society is the impersonalization of the vast majority of human relationships. Men do not meet as persons but as functionaries. All people wear symbolic, if not actual, uniforms to one another and meet as roles rather than as persons. It is much easier to exploit impersonal strangers than continuing neighbors. The accountability of sustained relationship is a reality to customers and clients in an intimate community context where one expects to spend his life, serving or working with the same people.

Coupled with the specialization of labor in many technical fields, the anonymity of the market provides an opportunity for widespread petty fraud. The nationwide surveys made by the *Reader's Digest* a number of years ago indicated that nearly three quarters of the automobile repairmen and radio servicemen would overcharge for work done or list repairs that were not made. In an increasing number of technical fields, where the average customer knows little about the mysteries of devices requiring service, there is an easy opening for such petty fraud. Most social scientists agree that in the impersonal life of mass society formal and legal controls become necessary to replace the informal controls of intimate folk society.

The mythology of business attempts to maintain the view that the overwhelming majority of men are wholly trustworthy in support of a purely self-regulative system, but the Christian perspective is less sentimental about human fallibility. Therefore, honesty is not something that can be left to the individual inner conscience, but must be supported by external patterns of approval and disapproval and lines of accountability. The Better Business Bureaus and business codes, even with no more than the sanctions of exposure to the public, are aids that support wavering human integrity and dependability. It is surprising to note how many business groups fight against the disclosure of weights, quantities, and ingredients on packaging, which could be one of the least coercive ways of increasing confidence and setting up simple guidelines of better business practice. Nearly all men plead honesty for the maintenance of reputation, but want loopholes for advantageous deviations. This generalization stands for clergy, ethics professors, and all the rest of us.

The trend from the folk society to the mass society reveals a significant paradox. In the folk society, individuals work for themselves and are economically independent, whereas the mass society moves toward heavy collectivism in the occupational world. Probably no shift has undermined the individualism of the early days of our history as much as the loss of occupational independence. One of the strongest convictions of Thomas Jefferson was that a free society could be maintained only if the majority of the people remained economically independent. This was why he placed so much faith in the free farmer or small shopkeeper who would be his own employer, and therefore, free from direct pressure from those who exercise the heavy sanctions of power over a man's livelihood. Jefferson's worst fears concerning the decline of the free occupations have come true.

Occupational dependence in our society now embraces the overwhelming majority of Americans. In 1860, the majority of our people were independent, while by 1960 approximately 80 percent of all breadwinners worked for others, predominantly in large bureaucracies. This organizational and occupational revolution has completely altered the context of economic organization.

This paradox of independence-in-community shifting to dependence-in-mass-society is illustrated in the field of social security. In the individualistic folk society, as practiced in rural America, there was a widely effective system of social security that operated as mutual aid. A farmer could have full confidence that in the event of illness or accident his neighbors would plant or harvest his crops; if his barn burned, the neighborhood would gather for a barn-raising. Today, however, only by dependence on public welfare and social security can a minimal security, under the greatly increased hazards of an impersonal employee-society, be restored.

THE ORGANIZATIONAL REVOLUTION

The most significant aspect of the big change and one that has far-reaching consequences upon our economic life is the "organizational revolution." It has turned us from a freeholder society to an employee society, from a society of dispersed power to one of concentrated power, and from an economy controlled by personal decisions to one controlled by corporate decisions. This has required massive new organizations of many types and a new army of administrators.

This change has made many aspects of the classical free-enterprise ideology inapplicable to the actual contemporary situation, and has also made the privatized or personal version of the "Protestant Ethic," developed in personal pietism, peculiarly irrelevant. More than anything else, it has changed the structure of economic organization so radically that it has obscured the lines of accountability and the regulative mechanisms to the point that they are at least partially inoperable. We are depending on a system of pressures and balances that no longer exists in its original form.

The giant corporation led the way into the organizational revolution and elicited the organizational response from many other groups. Vertical organizations, using the chain-of-command structure of the bureaucracy, as in the corporation, and many horizontal organizations have grown into the great "forest" of organizations that today dominates our economic world. Vertical organization orders people of dissimilar function and authority into a coordinated system, as in the corporation. In contrast, horizontal organizations are associations of men of similar occupation and function, developed for mutual protection and collective influence of the environment.

Organized labor is a conspicuous example of horizontal organization and is one of the significant organizations in the new power structure. Professional organizations were early comers in the process. The traditional professions of law and medicine have long been organized into effective organizations that have significant control over their members with disciplinary sanctions, ethical codes, and substantial influence on the educational and training requirements for the right to practice. Many new professions have come into existence with similar organizations and controls.

Trade and manufacturers' associations, huge farm organizations, and many others comprise what Professor Boulding calls the "vast jungle" of growing organizations. In turn, coordination and regulation of the "power group" society has called forth big government, which has the historic role of maintaining order and justice in the whole society. In an interdependent mass society, the competitive struggle has shifted from individuals to organizations.

The weight and voice of lone individuals in an urbanized society, in dealing with organized power groups, is almost infinitesimal. The reports of the Amsterdam Assembly of the World Council of Churches declared that one of the most difficult problems of our times is the plight of "the small man in a mass society." The sense of the helplessness of the average man to participate influentially in the processes that are determining his destiny is a source of great demoralization and passivity.

The organizational revolution has drastically changed the dominant decision-making process from personal decisions to corporate decisions. Individual persons are still participants; but instead of being personal negotiators and interrespondents, in a free market of decision, they now occupy roles as representatives of large aggregations. Prof. Robert A. Gordon, in his book *Business Leadership in the Large Corporation* (University of California Press, 1961), points out that decision-making in the large organization is substantially different. Organizational decisions are made under orders of predetermined policy at all lower and intermediate levels, or they are policy decisions made through compromise and reconciliation by the policy-making board or group at the top. This means that responsibility is dispersed. No one clearly shoulders the authority, even though this is technically borne by the chief executive officer.

PROBLEMS CREATED BY THE BIG CHANGE

It is possible to do little more than compile a brief list of some of the economic issues created by the revolutionary change.

1. Gigantic corporations are now vast centers of administration and control. Half of the manufacturing output in this country is produced by the one hundred and thirty largest corporations. General Motors is a bigger operation than the whole country of Yugoslavia. Such corporations exist as individuals under the law and are called private property holders. Their stockholders are so dispersed that they are no longer directly controlled by their owners. They often raise so much of their own expansion capital and are such blue-chip investments that banks can exercise little control over them. To whom are they accountable? This has become a question that is

raised by lawyers, social scientists, and economists, and by many candid administrators themselves.

2. Closely associated with corporate power is the increasingly blurred distinction between private and public administration. Harlan Cleveland has written an excellent description of this trend in *Bigness and Ethics* (Harper & Row, Publishers, Inc., 1962), which he edited with Harold D. Lasswell. Government is increasingly "farming out" large amounts of defense production, research, and actual administration to so-called private corporations who do much of the government's business. As government is called upon to do more coordination and administration by necessity and public demand, while faced with the unpopularity of increasing its bureaucracy, it lets contracts out to corporations whose operations grow bigger, so everyone is pleased. One of the primary economic functions that has been added to governmental responsibility is the task of keeping the economy stable and growing. The growing partnership between business and government in which business receives a large part of the taxpayer's dollar adds new complexities and problems.

3. Affluence, we have discovered, is not all promises but also perils. Some of these perils were indicated by John Kenneth Galbraith in his widely discussed book *The Affluent Society* (Houghton Mifflin Company, 1958). In an urbanized society, many of the scarcities that become more valuable are space, highways, recreation, and a more aesthetic atmosphere, yet these are goods that must be provided publicly; but we have a heavy prejudice against anything provided through taxation. The question is, Are we going to be compelled under the momentum of industrial production and advertising to buy more and more of what we least need just to keep the economy rolling?

4. Poverty is still an unsolved problem for a big block

of Americans, we are reminded by Michael Harrington in
his book *The Other America: Poverty in the United States*
(The Macmillan Company, 1962). There are still forty
to fifty million citizens who are deeply impoverished,
maimed, and defeated. In an affluent society, poverty
becomes more corroding not only to those who suffer it
but to those who ignore it. But the most serious problem
is that these people are becoming isolated and invisible
to the affluent majorities. They are in danger of becoming
a hard core of uneducated, unprepared, and self-perpetu-
ating people who will live wholly outside our opportunities
and incentives. This provides a set of urgent ethical issues.

5. The farm problem is another major economic issue
that has developed in the big change. Farming is a sector
of our economy made up of a large number of small units
(although rapidly decreasing) that can exert little control
on its own prices. Yet farmers buy indispensable ma-
chinery and many other goods at administered prices and
have the misfortune to produce a product concerning
which margins of surplus are a necessity for public safety.
As most agricultural economists agree, without subsidies
or production controls, agriculture would be permanently
depressed. If these are totally removed, a process would
take place that would probably force the family-size farmer
out of business and create a large-scale corporation-type
agriculture. Some people believe this should be allowed to
happen. Contemporary Protestant thinking, so far, seems
to feel that there are values to be preserved in the independent family-size farm. But here is a major issue with
many ethical ramifications.

6. Big labor unions are also a part of the big change.
Labor unions had a hard struggle to gain legitimacy in
America. They arose as a response to the impersonalization
of the labor market and the inequality of bargaining power
between a single man and a large organization. Protestants, as shown by denominational and council pronounce-

ments, have approved of labor organization since early in the century. However, labor unions, like all other organizations, have shown a vulnerability to corruption and self-interest, sometimes pressed beyond fairness. As Neil Chamberlain and other analysts have pointed out, the fear of labor as a monolithic power has undoubtedly been exaggerated.

These are only a few results of the big change that are indicative of new issues arising. They raise new ethical problems and dilemmas in the economic sphere. This study will not try to treat them or solve them. It will only indicate how they must be faced by Christians.

Chapter III

The Embattled Protestant Ethic

WHEN WILLIAM H. WHYTE, JR., THREW HIS BOOK *The Organization Man* (Simon and Schuster, Inc., 1956) into the intellectual market, it stirred up a controversial hornet's nest that is still buzzing. Neither the majority of businessmen who bothered to read it or its reviews nor the theological reactors to his version of the Protestant Ethic were exactly pleased with what they read. One sophisticated business group met in a series of discussions to consider its analysis of the organizational lives that they were leading. The reaction split the group roughly down the middle; one side vehemently rejected what they regarded as a caricature of life in the corporation, while the other side rather reluctantly saw at least a reasonable facsimile of the dilemma that they found themselves confronting. This dilemma was the problem of trying to work under a highly individualistic ideology in a tightly organized business bureaucracy. The group greatly admired and defended the Protestant Ethic, as Whyte delineated it, but conceded that it now bore little relationship or contained little guidance for their actual situation.

A group of historians and ethicists, grinding the same book through the mills of critical analysis, concluded that Whyte's popular version of the Protestant Ethic was little more than a ghost of the real thing, as they interpreted it from historic sources.

To Whyte, the Protestant Ethic is synonymous with what is often called "the American Dream" or "the American Way of Life." It is another designation for the idealized ideology of free enterprise. It is described as *"the pursuit of individual salvation through hard work, thrift, and the competitive struggle."* Its characteristics were *thrift,* saving more than is spent to increase capital to expand the economy; hard *self-denying work;* and a rugged *self-reliance* that is contemptuous of cooperation and collusion with others. He also recognizes that it had its rugged and stringent side that honored selfishness and the survival of the fittest, although this was sometimes partially hidden and rationalized in its lingering religious mythology. He further describes it as the "worship of individualism and the abhorring of all forms of collectivism which operate by group action, the suppression of individual creativity, and an anonymous type of corporate achievement."

He contends that a new orientation or ethic has displaced the traditional Protestant one. He labels it the "Social Ethic" or the "Organizational Ethic," which substitutes a new value system and moral justification for the dominating bureaucratic organization into which business enterprise has moved.

PROTESTANTISM: CHANGING YET THE SAME

It seems clear that this so-called Protestant Ethic, eulogized in the business world yet sick unto death in practice, is a highly secularized and stripped-down version, shorn of many of its genuinely Protestant meanings. Indeed, at several crucial points, it has become almost completely inverted and in opposition to its original Christian form. Therefore, a brief clarification of its basis, origin, and history seems necessary.

First of all, Protestantism is not a static set of moral principles that provide a constant formula, untouched by the dynamics of history. The very fact that its ethic became so mutilated in its secularized form is ample evidence of its changing character. As Robert McAfee Brown says in his book *The Spirit of Protestantism* (Oxford University Press, 1961), it is a spirit of openness to the renewing activity of God, who is always acting anew in every situation and age. The Reformation was not completed in the particular men or events of the sixteenth century, but continues as men submit themselves anew to the same Lord in their own contexts and dilemmas.

Protestants recognize that the "word" of God, his disclosure in Christ, must be retranslated into the vernacular of each new age and be rediscovered in each generation and, indeed, in each life. In their attempt to describe the basic characteristics of the Protestant movement, Dillenberger and Welch, in their book *Protestant Christianity* (Charles Scribner's Sons, 1958), remind us that "Protestant thought is a recurrent reinterpretation of Christian faith in response to new needs and situations." Therefore, it is a dynamic mode of responding to changing conditions and responsibilities as they are confronted in concrete decision. But there is a fundamental continuity that gives a shape and an identifying loyalty to the Protestant's solidarity and self-understanding. He stands in relationship to two poles: the text and the context; the constant "charter" of identification in Christ and the particular acts of faithfulness related to each unique situation. The danger of straying out of bounds is created by the necessity of cultural adjustment and reinterpretation. The danger of detached irrelevance is created by the call to abiding commitment to God-in-Christ, never to be broken. Only as these two identifications, in Christ and in context, are continuously recombined is faithfulness in action understandable and possible.

ALL IDOLATRIES REJECTED

Protestantism has been particularly fearful of all idolatries: the relative absolutes that usurp the place of God and become the recipients of ultimate fidelity. Protestant thinkers have been rather consistently sensitive to this temptation of misplaced absoluteness. The church itself has been one of the false pretenders to absolutism and infallibility and, therefore, must be kept open to criticism and continual reformation. Another type of false absolute to which Protestants have been vulnerable has been the verbal moral absolute that claims to represent eternal laws or specific behavioral rules that have been revealed in rational or Biblical legalisms.

Protestantism was a protest against the Roman Church's claim to be the only authentic interpreter of the natural law that God had created in the very structure of things. Both the specific requirements of natural law and various versions of divine law have often turned out to be cultural norms, developed in particular historical contexts and relevant only to passing frames of reference.

Man is not simply a creature of nature ruled by its iron physical laws and regularities, but is a self-conscious being who, in a limited fashion, selects and rearranges nature's energies. Therefore, from the Protestant perspective, no economic system can be defended on the basis of an infallible natural law. This is to resort to an economic idolatry and to declare historically relative arrangements to be eternal. It elevates an abstraction into dictatorship over the lives of men whether or not it serves their needs or creates a working balance of order and freedom. "The sabbath was made for man, not man for the sabbath." (Mark 2:27.)

Therefore, when the founding Assembly of the World Council of Churches in 1948 declared in its official report that "The Christian churches should reject the ideologies of both communism and laissez-faire capitalism and should seek to draw men away from the false assumption that these extremes are the only alternatives," it was remaining directly faithful to basic Biblical tradition. It was refusing to absolutize any economic system or exempt it from the necessity of continuous criticism and transformation under God. And it further recognized that no system is perfect or without basic internal contradictions and must continuously be revised as new and unpredictable situations make its former patterns obsolete. A rigid, unchanging system that fails to readjust to the new demands of radical social change is certain to be judged and shattered by a God who acts in history, who rules and overrules man's defensive obstinacies.

This does not mean that Christians are neutral or indifferent about the patterns of the economic system under which they labor. Indeed, as participants in it they seek unceasingly to direct its trends toward greater responsibility. The ethical advantages of our American patterns, of which the Christian is most appreciative, are its capacity to readjust to the changing power structures and produce a running self-criticism of disequilibriums that appear under changing conditions.

THE ORIGINATING REFORMATION ETHIC

The basic impetus of the rise of capitalism came from the demands of a rising new trader class that did not fit into the feudal structure. But it took a unique combination of many elements to create a whole new organization of the religious-political economy. We have recently gone through a period in which value systems and religious loyalties have been radically discounted, or dismissed, as causal factors in shaping history. However, as most contemporary texts on social movements insist, revolutionary movements do not spontaneously arise out of mere unrest and dissatisfaction. There also must be a set of focalizing ideas and purposes around which powerful motivations and loyalties are formed. These must be embodied in dramatic leaders with convincing interpretations of live issues. Luther and Calvin were preeminent examples of such challengers and reinterpreters.

They were not social revolutionaries or political and economic reformers. They were primarily concerned with man's redemption and his ultimate loyalty and destiny. They did not self-consciously launch or formulate a formal Protestant Ethic. The patterns of action that developed from their theological interpretations were derivative. These flowed from motivations and deep convictions concerning man's proper response to God's saving acts. These men were double respondents, as are all Christian reinterpreters of the Christian faith and its claims upon men. They were respondents to the historic situation in which they lived, which they regarded as corrupt and in discontinuity with the Biblical faith. And they measured this corruption and discontinuity by their even more focal response to the abiding source and center of their faith, the disclosing event of Christ as cradled in the Biblical Scriptures. This Christ revealed a sovereign God who had acted and intervened in history and demonstrated his unqualified love and everlasting concern for men, regardless of their merits or their just desserts. The great mediator was Christ himself, whom no sacred institution or law of life could usurp or appropriate for its own power or benefit.

Three guiding doctrines or convictions were enunciated out of this double response to what God-in-Christ asks in the crises laid bare in the context of the world.

THE SOVEREIGNTY OF GOD

First is the high and transcendent sovereignty of the God who creates, sustains, judges, and redeems; in whose hand all that is exists; and who acts and interacts in all moving events in his sovereign domain. No area and no dimension of activity is autonomous or immune from his guiding and transforming jurisdiction. Calvin carried this doctrine farther than Luther to its austere and logical conclusion.

From this, several Protestant themes of direct pertinence to economic life are derived. The Christian view of property holds that the world and everything in it belongs to God. This is the most radical view of property ever devised. Man basically owns nothing; he is a steward and custodian; a temporary trustee and assignee, under limited and qualified lease, who is called upon to return it unimpaired and with improvements. As one writer has put it, "The only true claim that a man can make that property is 'mine' is to actively recognize that he is God's." He is forever accountable in every use and every disposal to the Sovereign Lord of all. Furthermore, this Lord is not an absentee landlord or an innocent bystander who has made assignments "in perpetuity" and departed into retirement. He is actively in interaction in ongoing events, chastening and countering, transmuting blunders into less than total loss, and judging victories as less glorious than human pride believes.

ETHICS OF JUSTIFICATION

The second defining doctrine, enunciated by Luther and given concurrency by Calvin, was the doctrine of justification by faith and by faith alone. This was a denial of all forms of "works righteousness" or man's capacity to earn or merit salvation or to atone for his own sins through strenuous effort, good deeds, or absolutions. "We are not our own, we are God's." It is in this relationship that we have our being as selves. Grateful recognition of the belongingness of this ultimate relationship, this being grasped and rescued and pulled out of our defensive and inbound isolation, reorders and inverts the self. Moral action is not something that must be achieved in order to win the right relationship with God, but is the response of a "self" who is liberated and released by God's redeeming action. The good life could not be lived by man through self-discipline, self-seeking, or personal fulfillment, nor by conforming to natural or moral law, but only as he was touched by transforming grace and redeemed by God's saving mercy revealed in Christ.

Therefore, the Christian faith, stemming from the great reformers, is vigorously antimoralistic. In fact it is the great nemesis and opposition to all the carping moralism that parades under the Protestant banner. Moralism creates the embattled inner life in which with grim determination one attempts to whip himself into line, to compel himself to repress desires and spontaneities in conformity with all the legal restraints of the straight-and-narrow path. Such a person commits all his energies to the internal moral struggle. The more he turns the screw, the more embattled and compulsive he becomes. And, ironically, it is a battle in which victory is foredoomed because success is worse than failure. For if he manages to keep his list of negative proscriptions and to walk the tightrope within its narrow limits, undue pride in such a harrowing achievement is inevitable.

So the embattled moralist is trapped. The more petty victories he wins, the less he feels the need of grace and the action of God who brings the great release. In addition, the tragic impasse increases his hostilities to his less moralistic neighbors, whom he blames for their failure to fight the good fight. This, in turn, makes him more self-righteous and austere in crusading for more rigid laws and restraints that others may have the same unfortunate blessings that he discovers. Why should he carry the burden of righteousness on his shoulders while other men are immoral and free? Mercy and compassion, joy and creativity, have departed from his moribund life. And if he retains the sense that he is the true pilgrim and the faithful moral gymnast, he expects an appreciative God to reward him for his excruciating labors with the reward of eternal salvation.

This is one of the great inversions of the ethics of justification by faith into the corrupted Protestant ethic of justification by works. In its more secularized version, it does not take on quite this grim intensity. But many who feel emancipated from the Puritan tradition, which they interpret in the manner above, still are haunted by it and enmeshed in its moralistic web. Much of our humanism is simple moralism without recognition of the need of God's transforming action. It still includes the optimism of the moralist that he can deliver out of his own resources both the judgment and the discipline to stand ruggedly alone in the competitive world. He still believes that most men are trustworthy, if free, and is morally indignant toward all those "other people" who are hypocritical and blameworthy for undermining his profession or his organization.

Sin in Reformation Ethics

The Reformation doctrine of sin was not concerned with particular external deeds or with a casuistry or code of designated sins. The unit of ethical life was not the quality of the single act or the net accumulation of good or bad single acts. Instead, sin was a state of the whole self in its relation to God, whose grace alone provided the saving initiative and transformation. The Calvinists were even more severe with their doctrine of predestination under which the whole self is accountable in every moment and in every act. Man's salvation is wholly in God's hands and is known only by him.

The distinction between the sacred and the secular, the spiritual and the worldly, was displaced by the distinction of the elect and the lost. Under this rugged view, man was called to trust his destiny wholly to God with a willingness to be damned to his glory and his will. The Christian vocation was an expression of obedience to him and was utterly without effect upon winning God's favor. Therefore, it could find no motivation from sheer anxiety to save the self (this being already ordained, could not be at stake) but only from basic faith and fidelity in God's gift of grace.

How the Capitalist Breakthrough Happened

Max Weber, observing that it was in Protestant countries that the capitalist revolution made the swiftest headway and among Calvinists and Puritans that the preponderance of new entrepreneurs was developed, worked out his famous thesis. This thesis was that the Protestant movement was one of the principal solvents that broke up the sacred system of feudalism and provided a dynamic new alternative. It generated an intense new interest in science and technology. In one of the detailed histories of technology (Friedrich Klemm's *A History of Technology;* Charles Scribner's Sons, 1959) it is pointed out that, at the end of the seventeenth century, forty-two of the sixty-eight members belonging to the Royal Scientific Society in Britain were Puritans.

Calvinism provided not simply the new constituting ideas, which are a crucial initiating factor in all great movements, but an intense motivating faith. This faith of the new Protestants promoted a clear religious concern with activities and responsibilities in this world.

Weber calls this motivational contribution "worldly asceticism." It combined two usually contradictory motivations that made the new productive breakthrough possible, in what is W. W. Rostow's third *"take-off stage"* in his book *Stages of Economic Growth* (Cambridge University Press, 1960). These were intense and single-hearted devotion to hard work and production of goods, and frugal, prudent living—two characteristics rarely shown among comfortable middle-class people. In fact, it was one of the few middle-class movements in history. This is because the middle class, as aspiring emulators of the gentlemanly elite, have tended to adopt their contempt for work and abandon the grubby slavery of intense concentration on hard labor.

The takeoff stage requires an intense productive activity and development that rapidly creates wealth, but in addition a frugal plowing back of capital goods that are not consumed. This is one of the "neatest feats" ever accomplished, since it requires the rich to live like the poor and forgo the very benefits that presumably provided their incentives for the effort. It means saving and sacrificing, not simply for one's own future, but for the remote future beyond one's own life. This is exactly what the later free-enterprise reliance upon the profit incentive believed could not happen.

It is true that for the very rich, lavish luxury and heavy savings can both be accomplished, but not among the rank and file in a preaffluent stage. It is also true that the reward incentives could be for the wealth and affluence of children and grandchildren, but this does not account for the expected sacrificial life projected also for them. Calvinist prudence was not for this world, although it was exercised in it.

This combination of industry and thrift requires a value system and a faith that transcends the so-called incentives of individual material rewards and their immediate enjoyment. This is precisely what Calvinism contributed to the crucial breakthrough period: a doctrine of Christian calling or vocation that not only removed the Christian stigma and lack of full legitimacy of the medieval church toward material production but made it into a sacred calling—a ministry—to the glory of God and a ministry of Christ. It provided both a moral and sacred legitimacy, but even beyond that, a sense of holy and dedicated purpose.

In our highly secularized perspective, the vocational witnessing to the glory of God is easily viewed as pure hypocrisy, a divine alibi for other and ulterior motives. However, for the early Calvinists, in the dynamic period of this new and vital Christian movement when the conventional ways had to be abandoned for a conviction of faith, this is reading back too much modern cynicism. And the proof is in the strangely contradictory results of this wealth-gaining. It produced not a life of luxury and leisure but one of continued austerity and prudence for large numbers of people. Indeed, it framed the basic style of life to which they conformed. It was a serious fulfillment of a doctrine of stewardship that considered all wealth as a gift of God to be used frugally and responsibly.

The most important thing to remember is that Calvin and the early Calvinists were not setting out to construct a new economic order. They were theocratic and God-centered in everything that they undertook. They were interested in creating the Kingdom of God on earth of which God would be the sovereign ruler. Their emphasis in their unremitting labors was in faithfulness to God and the integrity of man in that devotion. Therefore, their influence on economic endeavor was wholly indirect and derivative. However, this fact does not reduce its actual impact.

The writings of many early Calvinists give evidence of their deep sense of accountability to God and a recognition of stringent ethical limits on how wealth was to be earned and expended. It is true that with time the strong emphasis on accountability became highly attenuated, secularized, and finally inverted.

The Weber thesis has been argued pro and con *ad nauseam* since its first appearance in 1904. But on the basis of contemporary scholarship we believe we can safely say that Protestantism and capitalism began as interlocking partners in the originating stages of our industrial order. This partnership was one of tension, but faith and economic life were recognized to be interactive. The next chapter will consider how separation then came about.

Chapter IV

The Reformed Ethic of the American Puritans

ON THE SHORES OF THE NEW WORLD, ANOTHER CHAP-
ter in the story was enacted with the typical tensions that
have always accompanied those who attempt to live under
the divine rulership while they struggle to subdue nature
and to compete with neighbors. The attempt to under-
stand this doughty band of our forebears has swung as
widely and extremely as the Weberian discussion. The
Puritans have been the alternate whipping boys and
heroes for both libertarians and authoritarians. Indeed,
like most stubborn men of scruples, they were both witch
burners and freedom bearers. They were men of strong
religious convictions who tried to enact their faith in the
setting of a "Holy Commonwealth" and in the sphere of
economic activity. Their contribution to our political
origins has been finely combed, but less so for their
economic legacy.

The Puritans in New England came with a fresh start,
not having to struggle with the authority of bishops and
kings of an old establishment. Therefore, at least until
they came into collision with their new and diverse
colonial neighbors, they attempted to express their convictions in their life-styles and the organization of their
community. Their motivating endeavor was to set up in
the new wilderness the Kingdom of God on earth. God

was to be their only King and the ruler of their lives. To this end they set up a holy commonwealth in order to live under God's initiative with three great Calvinistic convictions as their guidelines. These were: the sovereignty of God over all existence, the divine initiative as God's present rule in ongoing events, and the acute sense of human sinfulness. H. Richard Niebuhr (in his *Kingdom of God in America;* Harper Torchbooks, 1959), to whom we are gratefully indebted for this analysis, called this last guiding conviction "the principle of limitation" of earthly power. Under the necessity of having to establish these in the actual organization of a community, the Puritans discovered that the three often came into conflict and produced difficult dilemmas. Under a primary sense of the reign of God, active obedience and direct accountability to him for all their acts was their dominant concern.

This reinforced a type of individualism as personal response; but not one of individually isolated free men because all were bound in covenant to God, the only legitimate end to which their lives were to be directed. Therefore, "the kingdom of God was at hand" in the awesome "now." He governed all things directly, and the initiative and the goal were in his hands and not their own. Under God's rule, nothing happened that was not in relation to his providential guidance. His action took place, not in special events but in all the actual ongoing processes of reality, including economic life. But the divine will was discerned by those who saw the key of his action as revealed in God's saving and defining act in Christ. For this reason, the Puritans were very unlike the liberal Kingdom builders of a later generation of Protestants. Their understanding of the Kingdom was not dependent upon human action or human ideals. On the contrary, men were dependent on the Kingdom through God's acts. And his rule was not restricted to the inner consciousness, but to all institutions and patterns of life including economic pursuits.

In their refusal to recognize any worldly institution, including the church, or any legalistic code of morals as representing God's will without corruption, they confronted a great dilemma. How, then, could they organize and regulate political and economic life by referring to the will of God? If a man were emancipated from arbitrary restraints of trade and commerce, by church or kings, he might then make himself absolute and identify his own interests with God's interests. And if this were to happen, the Sovereign God would again be deposed. To renounce all rule but God's rule is to fall into confusion, but to liberate sinful and untrustworthy men to seek their own corrupt and inordinate self-interests is to fall into conflict and self-idolatry. Yet their acute sense of the sinfulness of man made them believe that men would surely abuse their freedom without restraint. For this reason they rejected the solution of later personal pietists who abandoned the restraint of power.

In the Calvinist tradition of Geneva and Scotland, the Puritans attempted to combine restraint with the limitation of restraint, an untrustworthy freedom with bondage in Christ. Aware that new usurping claimants to ultimate powers could rush into the vacuum left by the great church, they attempted to formulate a limited rule under which God alone would be judge and active Lord. They were high realists in their recognition of how relative and conditioned are human judgments, and how easily they become captive to special interests, whether they be political or economic.

The Puritans did not find it easy to institutionalize the rule of God in the patterns of their organized life. And at many points they went to extremes on the side of restraint. But as H. Richard Niebuhr pointed out, they did join two working principles from their Calvinist-Biblical antecedents: *constitutionalism* and *limitation of power*. And both of these have been woven into the American tradition in diverse ways.

CONSTITUTIONALISM

The constitution or charter of the Puritans, to which they turned under the pressures of decision in seeking for God's will, was God's revelation as found in the Bible. The Bible had been the charter of freedom of the Reformation, and the anchorage of trust against all powers claiming divine sanction. So God's own revelation in Christ could be the only steady pole of assurance in attempting to see God's will on the slippery new road they were treading. Both reason and conscience were easily corrupted by self-deception and could elevate man into pretentious sovereignty over God.

The Bible was the book of God's covenant with his people through Christ. Increasingly, the Puritans learned the hard way that it was not a specific law to be applied to particulars, but the source of their relationship to a God who has acted and still acts. Although they tended toward practical legalism, they resolutely maintained their belief in a living God who initiates and teaches through dynamic events. Therefore, as they confronted the concrete questions raised by their actual attempts to determine God's will, they carried on this dialogue with their "Christian constitution." This is the way they listened to the God who had spoken his word in Christ and speaks in present events. As Niebuhr put it, this "constitution was a record of a life not a law." It revealed a God who acts in the present, not simply in the past.

It is certain that they were not economic-determinists, but God-determinists because they believed that God was active in economic processes. As a corollary to the sovereignty of God, they firmly believed in the limiting of all earthly institutions and systems; and they began with the church. The church was not a voluntary association but a people of covenant, always returning to test themselves by their Biblical constitution. The church was not an object of faith or their moral authority, for only God-in-Christ could warrant that claim.

This Sovereign God who created, loved, and redeemed the world called his people out into the world to meet him in the arena of action and decision. This obedience, encounter, and accountability included all practical affairs and particularly economic life. In fact, in their Calvinist tradition, this part of their double vocation to serve God and to participate worshipfully in the world was of fundamental significance.

THE DOCTRINE OF LIMITATION

Next to the sovereignty of God, as its corollary, was the requirement of the limitation of all human power. Since all finite power has a universal tendency to absolutize itself and press its claims inordinately upon others, it must be restrained and balanced. As John Cotton wrote, "It is necessary . . . that all power that is on earth be limited, church power or other." It applied to all men, including the people of God, and all institutions and governments, including democracies. The Puritans were suspicious of power even in the hands of the people, because they feared that the common man could be easily misled and lured by foolish whims.

Roger Williams, a bolting but continuing Calvinist, declared "that free men are not Lords of their own estates but only stewards unto God." All these men, because of the very fact that they believed all men would abuse power, believed in legal restraints. Therefore, for precisely the same reason, they also believed in the limited power of all restrainers. And in the same vein they protested against the exercise of civil power by the church, and even New Englanders with established churches prohibited clergymen from holding civil office.

In their whole tradition, cutting across various divisions, Protestants have believed in the danger of power and the necessity of limiting it under the adamant insistence that only God is sovereign and absolute. Consistently, they have insisted on the finiteness and corruptibility of men, and have, therefore, maintained that conscience and reason are both not only subject to self-deception but can be the vehicles of its promotion and exercise.

All of this is so well known in connection with political life that it needs no documentation. However, in connection with the exercise of power in economic affairs, it is often obscured. What about the Puritan ethic in relation to business enterprise, since the Puritans are so often cited as the forerunners and fathers of the popular version of the Protestant Ethic in America? Were they completely myopic to the sovereignty of God over the economic affairs of men? Was the dialectic between the Biblical constitution and faithfulness to what God requires in every present decision irrelevant in this critical area of vulnerability to self-serving? The answer is clearly no! These Puritans made no exception in other areas of life. These men could not foresee the threats that would arise in the future. Economic power in their time was, comparatively, so dispersed and weak that it could scarcely occur to them that it should be specifically emphasized. In the modest trade and economic activity that did exist, they applied their full scruples in regard to honesty and responsibility as aspects of the faithful response to God in every economic transaction.

Richard Steele, writing in 1648, condemned "that notorious evil . . . to buy as cheap and sell as dear as they can." According to one quotation from Richard Tawney, profiteering was regarded as a scandal and was illegal in Boston. The same author summarizes the attitudes of early Calvinism in America by saying that it distrusted wealth and cast its scorn upon the rich and their riches because it corrupted the soul and distracted man from his true calling.

It is clear that, in the beginning and early stages, Calvinism and Puritanism, on both sides of the Atlantic, were theocratic rather than capitalistic, God-oriented rather than world-oriented, and preoccupied with the concern over how God's will was to be determined and man's sinfulness kept within bounds. Freedom was not the great obsession that it later became, because they believed that man is naturally a captive to sin and corruption and is truly freed only by standing in a new bondage in Christ through God's claiming action.

Nevertheless, the three great motifs of Reformed Protestantism were central themes in their self-understanding. These were: "calling," *"holy worldliness,"* and *"God's active rule."* They were on a chartered mission to which they had been called by God himself. This mission for their lives was "worldly," to be fulfilled in serving him in "a hideous and desolate wilderness" as he had opened the door of history for them.

THE SECULARIZATION OF THE REFORMATION-PURITAN ETHIC INTO THE GOSPEL OF WORK

The ethos of America, at the time of the Constitutional Convention, was still strongly tinctured with the understanding of the Reformed Ethic, no matter how detached from its Christian roots it had become. The framers of the Constitution showed in their writings and in the Constitution itself that the two great Puritan principles had survived: the principle of "constitutionalism" (covenantalism) and the principle of "limitation." But

one man was already laying the shape of the new secularized doctrine of calling. This appeared in the common-
sense creed of Benjamin Franklin. More than any other
of the founding statesmen, he was merging the congenial
elements of the Puritan heritage, bereft of its theological
basis, with the notions of *laissez faire.* The rugged and
simple gospel of work that he promoted was particularly
suited to a wilderness-taming, religiously illiterate, and
westerly moving generation of men. English liberalism
and rationalism provided a new rationale for the intel-
lectuals, while the practical men, preoccupied with exploiting a new continent, were too busy getting the job
done to spend much time in philosophizing. Theology in
New England, during the eighteenth century, had already
been adjusting away from the sovereignty of God toward
the self-sufficiency of man and from salvation by God's
action to salvation through moral striving and hard work.

The prosperous lawyers and traders had begun to lose
their consciousness of sinfulness, or their need for divine
grace, and were concentrating on worldly striving. Vocation was beginning to stand on its own feet with ample
worldly rewards as incentives. God became infinitely
benevolent, one who had created a wondrously good and
fruitful world in which man only needed to roll up his
sleeves and make the most of it. This world was ruled by a
natural law that governed the processes of things, and
God was no longer a ruling God in the world of events.
As H. Richard Niebuhr put it, the Kingdom of God dis-
solved into the Kingdom of Christ, who ruled only in the
inner consciousness of man to fill each soul with rejoicing.
The new Kingdom required the personal discipline of
honesty, sobriety, and the conventionally good life, and
allowed a double reward for merit—favor with God and
favor with men—as the fruits of hard labor. The transfer
of the focus of God's work to inner experience was to have
fateful consequences. It allowed the tragic separation to

take place in which faith was concerned in the inner sphere and the gospel of work could rule the outer world.

After the Civil War, the big change from the predominantly agrarian folk society toward the industrial urban society accelerated rapidly. The period of the industrial revolution moved into an intensive stage. The vestigial Puritan ethic that emphasized God's initiative and the free-enterprise ethic that emphasized human initiative were reinterpreted and merged into the "gospel of wealth." Through wealth, it was held, man can greatly extend his moral work. Acquisitiveness was glorified as God's greatest gift to man to motivate him to high and noble effort. Calvinism and the covenant theology of New England Puritanism, with its powerful belief in restraint and self-criticism, gave way to romanticism and the restriction of God's realm to the inner spirit of man. Mark Hopkins, a representative of his time, gave the essentials as: individualism, the sanctity of private property, and the duty of stewardship. Russell Conwell's lecture "Acres of Diamonds" was delivered six thousand times. He urged men to get rich as the test of their usefulness in the world. Bishop Lawrence of Massachusetts converted it into the test of morality and assured his contemporaries that wealth comes only in the long run to those with morality. "Godliness," said he, "is in league with riches."

It was Andrew Carnegie, a leading practitioner, who popularized the term *The Gospel of Wealth* in his essay and book by the same title. Carnegie argued that great organizers should reap big rewards and that an extreme deferential between the rich and the poor was the price of progress. However, he believed that to die rich was a disgrace, and he demonstrated this view of stewardship by giving his fortune away in hitherto unheard-of amounts.

The gospel of wealth picked up a powerful new ideological ally toward the end of the nineteenth century. This was social Darwinism as popularized by Herbert Spencer and vigorously promoted in America by William Graham Sumner, and even finally by influential clergymen like Henry Ward Beecher. Richard Hofstadter's *Social Darwinism in American Thought, 1860–1915* (University of Pennsylvania Press, 1944) is a fascinating account of the Darwinian influence on the dissolving Puritan Ethic.

Spencer took Darwin's biological theory of natural selection and converted it into a social theory in which "survival of the fittest" was applied to competition in the social and economic spheres. Out of it came the theory of automatic progress and an evolutionary view of history in which men and society were evolving from lower to higher forms through the process of selection. It was also converted into a view of ethical progress through the adaptation of character to the constantly improving conditions of life.

He held that human perfection is inevitable if the natural social process of competition and struggle is allowed full rein to follow its inevitable course. This was a brutal but inevitable struggle in which the costs of progress were the defeat and death of the weak and the supremacy of the strong. This became a magnificent doctrine to justify the free and unhampered pursuit of wealth and power by the great tycoons who were becoming fabulously rich exploiting the natural resources and defenseless labor provided by the tides of new immigrants.

This theory provided a basis for several of the doctrines of the gospel of wealth: (1) The doctrine of automatic technological and moral progress; (2) the doctrine that the strong, the wealthy, and the powerful deserve their strength because they are the superior and the fittest; (3) the doctrine that it is wrong to do good and pamper the weak because this hampers progress; (4) the doctrine that all reforms or attempts to plan or regulate the free life of individuals or economic affairs interferes with and thwarts the process of growth and progress; and (5) the view that the process of competition is the selector of the strong and the competent from the weak and the incompetent.

In fact its net effect was to make it wrong to do good to the unfortunate, unjust to help the poor, and misanthropic even to be a constructive critic. The demise and reversal of the Reformed view was virtually complete; the shambles that was left was christened with that euphemistic and wholly contradictory title "The Protestant Ethic."

The taming of the Reformed Ethic into the Protestant Ethic has been accompanied by parallel movements of Protestant protest. The Social Gospel movement was one of these. Its idealism was not in continuity with the Reformed Ethic in regard to its more optimistic view of the possibilities of a humanely developed Christianization of economic life. It brought disillusionment to many of its members. On the whole, it was rejected by the laity who found it abstract and ivory-towered.

A new theological movement has turned to a reexamination of our Biblical-Reformation sources. It attempts to restore the sovereignty of God as revealed in Christ and the realistic view of human nature. It sees again the world as the arena of God's action and man's response in all of his activities.

Chapter V

The Business Ethic and the Reformed Ethic

IN ORDER TO MAKE A CAREFUL COMPARISON OF THE contemporary American business creed with the basic Reformed-Protestant tradition outlined in prior sections, let us list the creed's chief characteristics. This list is derived from many resources. Particularly well documented is *The American Business Creed,* by Francis X. Sutton and three colleagues (Harvard University Press, 1956), in which an elaboration of these characteristics is given. They are: (1) central emphasis on the individual; (2) self-reliance; (3) productivity: volume of material production as the chief measure of well-being; (4) activism as the most honored way of life; (5) progress as chief goal and hope; (6) optimism as the only valid personal and historical attitude; (7) competition as the key regulator of the economic system; (8) consumer sovereignty as ruler of production; (9) self-interest or "the profit motive" as the decisive incentive in human effort.

This is the traditional list of attitudes and requirements underlying the operation of the free-enterprise economy, as developed in its independent secular phase and as promoted today by its traditional ideologists. There is now a whole wing of the business community that recognizes that this combination of attitudes is not adequate for a responsible economy in a radically changing society. This less doctrinaire and more realistic group is self-consciously asking many critical questions. They are recognizing that there are many new dilemmas arising in economic life, and that ethical judgments that go beyond profit-and-loss factors are involved in all decision-making. This trend toward realism in business, coupled with the new recognition of the importance of facing concrete facts in Christian ethics, is creating the new convergence of practical action and ethical reconsideration. This is making a new possibility for creative dialogue between Christian ethicists and those with practical business responsibility. Let us compare the basic Christian view with the business creed under these considerations.

INDIVIDUALISM

All scholars seem to agree that "rugged individualism" has been one of the primary motifs in the American business creed from the time it began to shake free from its theocratic foundations. One of the important bases of this individualism has been the psychological atomism that stems from the eighteenth-century views of Rousseau, Locke, John Stuart Mill, and Adam Smith, which is now rather thoroughly discredited in the behavioral sciences. It is the notion that individuals have their own ironclad inner characteristics, entirely unaffected by relationships, and that organizations are only the combined characteristics of the individual members with nothing added by the organizational structure. It, in fact, denies the reality of social organizations and culture systems and their conditioning influences upon human individuals.

Today, widely accepted theory sees men as "persons in community" where the process of interpersonal interaction is the matrix in which the human self is developed and exists. Between atomic individualism and collectivism stands the interactional theory in which the truly differ-

entiated and self-conscious person cannot exist or develop
genuine individuality at the pole either of isolation or of
absorption in a collective. A completely introverted person, that is "individualistic" in the sense of being non-
interactive, is called psychotic from a psychological point
of view. As most social psychologists would put it, a fully
individuated individual is not a human person. The dis-
tinctive life of persons is the life of dialogue in which a
process of identifying with others and responding back to
the self takes place.

In spite of its claim of being individualistic, however,
the business creed implicitly concedes that one of the
chief facts of life about economic activity is the negotiating
market or arena of interchange. Among the significant
agreements between Protestant thinking and the business
creed is this recognition that man is in fact an interactive
creature, responding and being responded to; negotiating,
trading, and bargaining not only of material goods in the
economic process of exchange, but of ideas, fears, and
appreciations. Sharing and competing are the two sides of
this process.

There is a cardinal insight about man in the dynamic
notion of the world as a marketplace of continual exchange. To many Christian moralists, the use of this
crass commercial term for the whole interpersonal arena
of life may seem shocking; but it comes closer to a description of a cardinal fact about the common life of men
than many of the static notions of philosophical theoreti-
cians. Furthermore, it is true that all participants gain in
many of the transactions and there does not have to be a
loser or an exploiter and an exploited. However, it is also
true that the point of interaction is also the point of
highest opportunity and temptation to take advantage of
the other man.

Let us ask, What is the Protestant-Biblical view of
individualism? In a valid sense, Protestantism is individ-

ualistic in that it has held that every individual self stands in relationship to God without the necessity of institutional mediation. Christ, as presented in the Bible, is the only mediator necessary. As Luther insisted, every man has to do his own living and dying, and his own responding to God's saving act in Christ.

The Biblical covenant theology always sees the human individual as encountering God's will in the context of concrete circumstances and as a member of the covenant people. Ralph Barton Perry (in *Puritanism and Democracy,* p. 312. The Vanguard Press, Inc., 1944) maintains that Puritan theology tended toward individualism because the elect felt that they individually belonged to a select and privileged body that prepared them for salvation without their fellows and even without their loved ones. This, he believes, tended to harden the Puritan's heart and make him a rugged individualist without the need of fellows or church or even concern for neighbors. However, we must conclude that this represented an advanced state of secularism, because Calvinist tradition saw love and service to neighbor as a fruit of the grace-filled life, and held a crucial place for the covenant community as the people of God.

Covenant theology was both personal and corporate, for it provided a common bond that joined the people of God with one another. The church, founded in Christ, was the new covenant people. Perry Miller (in *The New England Mind,* Vol. 2: *From Colony to Province.* Beacon Press, Inc., 1961) says that there was no suggestion of individualism in Puritan thinking from the standpoint of a private inner relationship with God. Economic life, no less than the life of worship, is lived under God's covenant rule and in response to him. As one seventeenth-century Puritan essay, which was printed and reprinted, stated, "Man was made for society."

SELF-RELIANCE

Closely related to individualism in the honored virtues or attitudes of the moral code of the classical American business creed is self-reliance or independence. One of Benjamin Franklin's maxims was, "God helps them that help themselves." It has been said that the most popular cult in America has been the "cult of the self-made man" who, by sheer pluck and determination, rose from poor and humble beginnings to power and wealth.

This is obviously unrealistic concerning all men, and particularly in an increasingly interdependent society where single individuals are almost totally impotent unless they work in and through large organizations which coordinate the work of large numbers of individuals. The driving entrepreneur is a disappearing breed in an economy where success is dependent on an organization of specialized experts and an efficiently functioning organization. As William S. Whyte rightly perceived, managers and administrators cannot be individualists.

From the side of the Calvinist-Puritan mode of thinking, self-reliance is almost the direct antithesis of its main tradition. Self-reliance is almost a direct synonym for pride and obstinacy and the denial of the need of grace from beyond the self.

Ralph Barton Perry has suggested that the only gratuity that the Puritan enterpriser would accept was salvation and dependence on God because this enabled him to be independent of his fellowmen. This is the use of other-worldliness in order to be more irresponsibly this-worldly. This is obviously a high perversion of the original view of dependence on God for one's very existence and the unavoidable encounter with him in every decision in this world. To the less secularized Calvinist or Puritan, nothing could have seemed more sacrilegious than this.

PRODUCTIVITY

One of the disagreements often revealed in discussion between Christian ethicists and practical businessmen is over the importance of productivity. The latter often say that the ethicists have been so preoccupied with how the pie is to be cut up and distributed that they show little concern for increasing the size of the pie for more ample shares. To have a strong incentive to produce a bigger pie, inequities are considered inevitable and necessary.

Realistic Christian thinking must agree that an equitable distribution of poverty is not a way to meet human need. Furthermore, management and men of power are indispensable to organize and coordinate an intricate industrial system and must be given legitimacy and be expected to gain greater rewards for their risks in decision-making. These risks are now not so much the risks of capital, since most managers work largely with other people's money, but are the risks of laying one's reputation, position, and future on the line as living collateral. Few people would want the risks of top leadership if it were all "headaches" with no rewards.

The Christian is compelled to hold that both increased production and fairer distribution are necessary and must be kept in balance. A society and its economy that would make its rich people richer and its poor people poorer would demoralize both and move toward catastrophe. The best argument that Americans have against communism is that its gloomy predictions that capitalism would produce this trend have not come true. An affluent society, in order to be sensitive to the supremacy of persons over things, must press for a realistic policy for overcoming impoverishment at the lower levels.

Sheer production of material goods or volume of sales transactions, however, must not be given supremacy under the Christian perspective. "Production for what?" a question once framed by Clarence Randall, the former steel executive, must be continuously asked. How can we escape his conclusion that material production must always be instrumental to a higher destiny of man or it is "merely treading water."

ACTIVISM

American activism, one of the chief characteristics eulogized by the business creed, has often been ridiculed by our European colleagues. This criticism often implies that quietistic contemplation is a superior preoccupation of man. However, this stands more in the classical Greek tradition or in the mystical line of Christianity than in the Reformed-Protestant tradition. Rightly understood, this activist orientation may very well be more faithful to the Biblical-Reformed understanding. The Christian faith, as already indicated, does not consist of dry beliefs but of responsive acts. It is a religion of verbs: responding, acting, witnessing, serving, meeting. Man is an active and interactive being, and to be anything less is not truly human. In the internal contradiction, within the business creed, of the "quietistic self versus the man of action," authentic Protestant theology is on the side of action. However, it does not honor action for its own sake but insists that the question be completed. To whom is the basic response to be made? To whom do we witness? To what end and purpose do we act? In whom is genuine vocation meaningful? Active and interactive man is lost at sea, alienated and cut off from the creative and sustaining source of his life, if these questions are left dangling. Man's life is sustained and authentic only in the "alterctive" dialogue in which God is acting and man is responding. This is the relationship that Christ revealed in his full response to the Father.

PROGRESS AND OPTIMISM

The Christian is optimistic along with the business creed, but it is a radically different kind of optimism. It is in continuity with its Calvinist-Puritan source rather than with the social Darwinism that so drastically diverted the Christian meaning. Christian optimism is based on trust and fidelity in the God revealed in Christ. It has no faith, as do both "business creeders" and communists, in the sure and inevitable progress of history or the confidence that human effort can solve man's perennial conflicts. The more man taps the atomic secrets of physical power and devises machines to do his work and calculating, the closer he may come to his own destruction unless greatly increased responsibility is developed.

The most threatening aspect of the technological and organizational progress is that small blunders, which men inevitably make, are now geometrically multiplied into chain-reacting catastrophes. To live in the new world that can no longer afford mistakes, yet one operated by ordinary mortals filled with selfish prejudices and deep hostilities, is hardly reassuring. Many human blunders are made with perfect confidence that they are brilliant plans.

Let us take an example of a small blunder, uncritically executed in the middle 1950's by a small group of men working in their designer's studios. In the interests of creating a sleek new salable model of the motorcar, they lengthened it on an average of slightly less than two feet, and all the manufacturers used their elongated design. It was not done out of hostility or a grudge against their fellowmen. Yet this small blunder cost other men billions. Several experts have tried to make estimates, but no one knows the real costs, although it is certain that they were astronomic.

Suddenly it took 18 percent more parking space for

millions of motorcars. To the downtown areas of cities, already hard pressed for space, it was an added blow. Businesses went bankrupt; buildings were torn down to make way for garages; stores abandoned their historic downtown locations and moved to expansive new shopping centers; people had to lengthen their garages. Downtown areas of cities went into decline and property lost value. Was the longer automobile progress? Yes, for the steel-makers; no, for urban property owners.

Acute sensitivity to behavioral consequences is more ethically important than ever before. Specific gains can be made through human decision and planning by alert and sensitive men. Furthermore, they can be institutional-ized into organizations when new alternatives open. But they are never secure or without need of revision. Hope that is secure lies only in God's hands. He is the initiator; we are the respondents.

The optimism that the business creed seems to promote is a state of mind that is open to serious question and con-tradicts the spirit of classical Protestantism at one of its most essential points. This business attitude of positive thinking and the suppression of thoroughgoing self-criti-cism is perhaps the greatest departure from its Puritan sources. Wishful thinking is hardly congruous with the kind of Puritan realism that business still likes to claim. W. J. Cameron, who was the radio spokesman for the Ford Motor Company for years, called it "a rule" that "we are thinking wrongly unless we are thinking hope-fully." The view that one is "antibusiness" if he is not citing the glories of our economic system shows its deepest vulnerability. This is credulous and sentimental self-delusion, not true loyalty.

Self-criticism, by the grace of God, is the very heart of the Protestant spirit and ethic. The confessional that we are "wrong men" and that we need forgiveness and continuous new light to recognize more responsible possibilities and to learn from every past mistake is not an option for the Christian. The fact that the churches have not been able to communicate this spirit to their people is one of the most humbling evidences of failure or of the triumph of the secular spirit. The churches, themselves, have begun to recapture this spirit of continuous reformation; and if they can become their own most vigorous self-critics, under God, perhaps their members can begin to apply this self-criticism to other aspects of life.

COMPETITION

Competition is the anchor concept of the business creed and its most controversial doctrine. There is need of hardheaded Christian realism in the analysis of the actual state of competition in modern corporate society. Economists and professors of business administration are, on the whole, demonstrating this kind of realism. But many leaders in the business community feel compelled to defend it in new ways even after it has lost its key function as pricing regulator. The mechanism of competition has had to carry the complete burden of regulating and balancing the complex apparatus of business; pricing, product design and selection, expansion of productive capacity, and capital financing, presumably, are all to be regulated by the process of competition. It has even been made to carry a substitute function for the ethical judgment. All these things are to be determined as responses to the barometer of the market.

But if the essential conditions necessary to keep a genuinely free market in operation no longer prevail, then the equalizing pressure system falls into disequilibrium and can no longer perform its imperative functions. Yet the decline of competition seems to be the most important single economic fact of the organizational revolution.

No single strand of the Puritan tradition seems to have survived in the secularized value system more fully intact than the fear of unbalanced power. Therefore, the decline of competition has left a vacuum in the power structure that exposes many industries and organizations to challenge on the basis of our basic value system. The result has been for the ideologists of the business creed to shift their definitions and proofs of continuing competition in order to plead the case against new forms of accountability. There are new forms of countervailing power in our organizational structures, such as labor unions, large corporate buyers, and retailing chains. But no automatic balancing mechanism can be assured out of these because the power of groups varies.

In many fields, "administered pricing" seems to be rather strongly institutionalized and this does place substantial economic power in the hands of the decision makers in these fields. Price competition has been largely abandoned in the "concentrate" industries, to use A. A. Berle's term, in which a few large corporations dominate the market. There are very good reasons for this trend: to avoid business fluctuations, to stabilize production, to keep employment levels steady, to avoid freezing out small marginal producers, etc. Very important values are preserved by administered pricing that may well be to the advantage of large majorities. But rather than argue these advantages, many business groups choose to argue against the realities of administered pricing in which they participate and whose advantages they enjoy.

The case of the conspiracy of the electrical manufacturers shook the business community to its foundations because it clearly revealed a widespread practice in contradiction to its most sacred principle. Now several similar cases are running through the courts. In the electrical manufacturers' case, a serious ethical conflict was exposed.

Some of the corporations involved, during the very period that they engaged in price collusion, were also promoting expensive public relations campaigns to convince the American people that free enterprise is the most effective economic system and that its operation depends upon competition. Instead of arguing the economic advantages and ethical justification of administered prices, which are many, they chose to eat crow and save the corporate image by compounding the hypocrisy by firing top men who were carrying out company policy. This case clearly illustrates the necessity of institutionalizing ethical responsibility. As Judge J. Cullen Ganey pointed out, in his conclusions before sentencing the convicted electrical conspirators, these men were torn between conscience and corporate policy. It will not do to use the old alibi that these men lacked moral character when they operated under this pattern and pressure. The value system and the lines of accountability were shown to be inadequate. It is clear that there are values to which many corporations give higher priority than to competition. This value conflict is the heart of the dilemma, not a few "bad apples in the barrel." Since the company found these men after long experience to be the type that could carry out the actions it demanded, it is doubtful that they suddenly became unreliable.

Today, much of the administered pricing is out in the open and requires no collusion whatsoever. In "concentrate" industries, the recognized price leader simply raises his prices and others follow. In many states fair pricing laws have made it illegal for retailers to engage in competitive price-cutting. Many industries now operate under stable pricing. One of the results that proves the demise of price competition has appeared in several of our business recessions. It is what some of the economists have called "inflated recession." In a period of declining sales, instead of reducing prices, they are raised while production is cut back. Under the classical model of economics, this is an impossibility without price agreements.

It now seems doubtful that market competition has ever been the neat regulator that has been claimed or that it can alone provide "the limits" necessary for responsible business administration. There are crucial ethical issues here to be worked out by responsible men who are willing to combine economic and ethical considerations.

CONSUMER SOVEREIGNTY

One of the most important doctrines of the classical business creed is that the consumer is king and makes the basic decisions that govern what is produced in the economy by acceptance or rejection on the market. Therefore, the producer never has to make moral judgments concerning what is good or bad for others. He simply offers his goods or services, and awaits the acid test of acceptance or rejection from the potential customers.

Every purchase is a vote toward determining the basic priorities that shall rule the culture. Therefore, ethical responsibility in buying should be taken seriously by Christians as one of the key areas of decision concerning the kind of world we approve. The statistical analyses that have indicated how the American people spend their money reveal some weird and almost preposterous indexes on American desires and tastes. Perhaps an annual chart on what we buy would be a salutary disclosure. Shouldn't a people be given the returns on how their votes are going, who the productive winners are, and how cigarettes are polling against education?

However, when we give a closer look at consumer sovereignty, we discover that the election is not completely fair in a technological-organizational society. No longer does the consumer quite get to see the product in the bright containers, and he doesn't have the technical competence to judge its quality. Misrepresentation directly and by creating illusion is widespread, and there is a multi-billion-dollar advertising industry engaged in tampering with and rigging the consumer's best judgment.

There seems to be a big segment of American industry that insists on the right to practice fraudulency on the impersonal market. Why should so many business leaders be against the Truth-in-Packaging Bill or measures to require a disclosure of simple interest rates in installment selling, or rigid testing and labeling requirements on foods and drugs before they are sold to a trusting public? Why do many respectable executives believe that protecting and promoting true consumer sovereignty would spell the ruin of free enterprise?

Here there are some very serious ethical issues involved. From the classical Protestant perspective it is not surprising that good men will practice fraud if there are easy loopholes. It has consistently taken the realistic side as over against the romantic side, advocated by many in the business world. This is why Christians seek stable patterns and open disclosures to keep themselves in line. If consumer sovereignty is both good business and good ethics and is going to be given a chance to function, then full disclosure is necessary. Valid competition cannot be based on misrepresentation, but must be based on price, quality, and service. One of the most legitimate functions of government in the theory of the philosophers of classical free enterprise is to protect its citizens against fraud and theft. If a way could be discovered to add even a fraction of the cost of advertising to the price of products to pay for testing laboratories and full disclosure reports, we could have more assurance concerning the future of our free economy. In this field, facts would be more powerful than penalties, and would honor freedom rather than compulsion.

SELF-INTEREST

The classical Protestant view agrees with the business
creed that self-interest is a universal characteristic of
human beings and must be recognized in both ethical and
practical considerations. However, it remains constantly
realistic while the business creed turns sharply romantic
concerning how self-interest actually motivates man. The
Calvinist-Puritan motif of "limitation" was lost in the
secular romanticizing of the Protestant Ethic during the
nineteenth century. This is the doctrine of accountability:
no man is trustworthy unless held accountable. Self-
interest must be clearly understood for what it is—a
radical kind of introversion and narrowness of outlook
that creates self-deception and defensiveness. The fact
that it is a permanent aspect of the human self means
that it must be constructively utilized and directed. Restraint must be both inner and outer—that is, within
persons and within the patterns of organizations.

The primary difference between the old Reformed
Ethic and the new Protestant Ethic revolved around the
meaning and method of gaining freedom. To the former,
man was already enslaved and required liberation: something he himself could not accomplish and which could
be found only in a new bond of commitment to, and
dependence upon, God. The latter was romantic to the
core and believed man to be naturally free, and, therefore,
resisted all community claims on the self and all the
pressures of accountability. His freedom was the freedom
of anarchy, one adopted by Marx for the final stage of
communism after men were coerced out of their enslaving
institutions.

But the Reformed Protestants affirmed the doctrine of
"the continuing sin of the redeemed." The freedom of a
man in a vacuum, outside the context of community and

without the continuous claims laid upon him by God, would have seemed totally beyond comprehension.

The most dangerous consequence of celebrating and singing hosannas to self-interest is that it destroys man's capacity for self-criticism and self-transcendence and therefore of creativity. It is one thing to recognize realistically the self-interest in all human beings, in order to direct it into constructive channels and submit it to transformation and restraint, as does the uninverted Protestant view, but something else to elevate this inversion into a glorious virtue in its own right. It is not something to be cultivated and esteemed, but something to be guarded against and transcended within the highest limits of possibility. A human being who is not continuously on guard against self-deception and his own compulsive biases will be crippled and chained. His perception and interpretation of situations and the claims of others will be faulty. His capacity for learning and appreciation will be impaired and shriveled.

Some of the examples of the great entrepreneurs are excellent case studies of what happens to the man who becomes a megalomaniac. The total preoccupation with self-aggrandizement produces the destruction of the self. A man whose relationships become exploitive, who takes maximum advantage of others in every transaction, who asks only one question, "What is in it for me?" is a man on the road to self-isolation and psychological deterioration. Most modern psychiatric interpretations will document this fact about human behavior. They would call it retrogression from maturity or reversion to the infantile. In terms of the Christian faith, it was what Jesus' great warning question was about: "For what does it profit a man, to gain the whole world and forfeit his life?" (Mark 8:36.)

Self-interest always is dangerously compounded when

operating in powerful organizations. It is easier for a General Motors man to believe that what is good for G.M. is good for the nation than it is to believe that what is good for me is good for you. When large groups celebrate their loyalty and common identification, it becomes a kind of narrow patriotism under which disloyalty reaps corporate scorn and disapproval. The big bureaucracy tends to develop yes-men who show enthusiasm in expediting the standard policy and moralizing its legitimacy in order to gain advancement.

The most important thing to be said must be cast in the form of a question that can be answered only by experience: Is it possible for large organizations to develop self-critical men who can be ethically creative toward discovering new institutionalized forms of responsibility? Christian commitment requires nothing less. Is there any power in God's grace that makes this possible?

Chapter VI

Convergence in Decision

THE DEAN OF A WELL-KNOWN SCHOOL OF BUSINESS administration has said that the problems of business ethics are not to be found in the university but out in the area of business. We hasten to add that neither are they to be found in churches or in the books of social ethics professors, but only out where the actual decisions are encountered. The concrete decision is the point of intersection between faith and action, between responsibility and possibility.

We have discussed the divergent histories and assumptions of the secular business creed, the changing forms of Protestant ethics and the tragic separation that developed between the two. We believe that there is now a new convergence sufficient to allow a new dialogue. The seekers for ethical guidelines in business recognize again that our economy is not self-regulating. Christian ethicists have been reexamining their Biblical-Reformation sources and have come to recognize that defending abstract ideals or pointing to inflexible moral absolutes is neither good theology nor meaningful ethical advice.

The hopeful point of convergence from both sides is *the decision,* the unit where Christian fidelity and economic responsibility meet.

ELEMENTS IN THE DECISION

Let us look at the elements that make up the decision. First is the situation or context in which the decision is confronted. This is the gestalt or the actual set of circumstances, including the interrelated human beings involved, the organizational structure in which the decision is laid, the actual alternatives that are possible, the particular issues at stake, and so on. Ethical situations come ready-made with many possibilities already foreclosed and with many limits already imposed from the past. One of the frustrations about human decision is that ideal situations never exist; there are no fresh starts. Ethical situations often arrive as "messes" to be straightened out, heavy pressures to be balanced, or opposing values to be weighed. The obstinate idealist can usually offer only the helpless and hopeless advice "that such a bad situation should never have been allowed to happen."

Ethical situations have varying degrees of complexity. Some of them may be so intricate that an understanding of the facts requires technical advice from many other people. One of the most important ethical requirements is to know the facts as far as possible, since these are always a part of the ethically significant ingredients of a situation. This is why the ready-made answer can never be fully responsible.

Solving all problems by formal routines is one of the great threats to genuine responsibility in an organizational world. Every big organization must have a set of formal regulations ("the book"), according to which much routine can be carried out just as individuals need habitual routines to live an ordered life. But to have the sensitivity to know when book answers are inadequate and unfair is one of the important requirements of ethical decision-making. There can be no substitute for an indefinable quality, called the capacity to see all the elements and factors involved; and this can be developed only in experience. This is why the case study method is necessary for the development of both good managers and good ethicists. Good management and good ethics involve the same factors in the same situations.

The failure to see the ethical significance of all the personal and technical factors of the situation has created much of the sterility and irrelevance of Christian ethical thinking. This means that there can be no absolute and inflexible moral code that provides right answers to moral issues before they are confronted. And, for the Christian, it means that there is no code that spells out God's will for man by sheer formula. Formula-guided acts are not genuine decisions; they are repetitions. Machines are now often superior to men in this field.

What Does the Christian Faith Provide for Decision-Making?

What does the faithful Christian take with him into the situation of decision? It is now clear that he does not take a set of galvanized behavioral absolutes with him. Moral absolutes are either so abstract and generalized that they are empty of meaning or they are so specific that they will do violence to the unique situation. Furthermore, a man who believes he has a set of such absolutes, particularly if they are thought to represent divine commandments, will be obstinate and unyielding to the claims and ethical judgments of others. He will be unable to be a man of synthesis and reconciliation; he can only be a moral dictator with the specially obnoxious characteristic of claiming to know God's will.

A far more important thing that the Christian takes with him into the ethical situation is "the committed self."

The Christian as committed self believes he stands in relationship and in accountability to the only nonidolatrous absolute that the Christian worships and encounters with his whole being. This is the Sovereign God, revealed in the Christ event, who rules and overrules all existence, including every decisional situation. The Christian recognizes two things about himself that are of crucial significance to his decision-making. First, his own judgments are finite and conditioned by his own background, prejudices, and hostilities, which must continuously be corrected and transformed. And, secondly, the mode of this transformation is one of the greatest importance. The "separationist," as we have called the man who suffers the fatal split between his faith and his actions, is likely to think that he needs to rush off to church in detachment from all of the elements of the ethical situation and call on God for a mystical vision or the still, small voice. This reveals a fatal misunderstanding and shows how far we have defected from the Reformed Ethic.

God acts in and through the decisional event itself. This is where he is encountered; this is where the ethical claims and responsibilities converge. This is where the sensitivity of perception, the synthesis of all the elements, the judgment of consequences, are met with urgent and inescapable directness. This is a return to the sovereignty of God in and over all historical events, where he is acting to open possibility, to intensify recognition, and to lay concrete claims on his respondents in the crucial time of accountability.

How can modern men see God acting in ordinary events and what do they see that is any different from what nonreligious men see? This is, of course, a difference in perspective, in focal commitment. It is a difference in the "reading" of the situation and the claims and possibilities that are sensed and accepted. God speaks to man in two coordinated ways, through the "text" and the "context." The text is the "word" of God enacted in Christ, who is the revealing event through whom the Christian finds his identifying "location" in existence. Each new "context" is the event in which God is reenacting his creating and redeeming work for those whose self-defining loyalty is constant. The Christian is a respondent to what God has done and is doing to elicit new responses to concrete possibilities in each unique time and place. Faithfulness is not abstract but particular; it is not static but dynamic; it is not repetition but true decision. The Christian is called to be a true man after Christ in the *kairos*, the fullness of time that God has brought forth for man's full and undefensive response to the situational possibilities. This is the defining difference between the so-called moralist and the Christian decisionist. The first attempts to be faithful to laws or rules laid down by others in their time and place; the second must stand in his own personal situation and respond.

The Christian ethic is always a do-it-yourself call into action, not a do-what-someone-else-did in repetition. The Christian is likely to see more, recognize more significant alternatives and their ways of enactment. This is how the Christian is the most religiously bound (in the ultimate relation) and the most ethically free to risk unique decision.

This description has been highly personal, in a sense individualistic, but it is also intensely social. Let us turn to this social side of decision-making. Most of the decisions in the economic sphere are cooperative decisions. They are reconciliations of many points of view and many interests within the ingroup in which policy is formed and of which individuals are representatives. Many decisions are also negotiations with outgroups, which take place in mutual bargaining with other men or organizational representatives. Selling or buying property, goods, or services is the characteristic transaction of the economic sphere. Although each side seeks the most advantageous bargain that can be obtained, it is the standard presupposition of a free market system that a business transaction should be advantageous to both parties of a contract.

In an organizational world, ethical problems arise because of the differential bargaining power between groups, created by the urgency of need, control of supply, and many such factors. The question concerning whether maximum advantage should be pressed when negotiating with those in a weak or desperate position raises an ethical issue of great significance. Should the opportunity to take excessive advantage of a weak bargainer be exploited to the utmost? On the basis of pure self-interest in competition the answer is yes, but from the Christian perspective this cannot be the final criterion.

Two considerations will infuse the perspective of the Christian bargainer that will motivate him to transcend the sheer seeking of maximum self-advantage. First is the recognition that other persons have an ultimate status in relationship to God and a claim upon the self that cannot be denied by the Christian. This is the basic Christian recognition of the supremacy of persons over things and, therefore, they are never to be reduced to exploitable resources. Many Christian ethicists would call this the law of love or the supreme Christian ethical principle, but we hesitate to state it in this fashion, for Christian love is not an abstraction, nor is it reducible to an external commandment. It is the capacity to rise above self-defensiveness and self-serving, which no rule or law can produce, nor self-discipline create. Grace alone brings it to those who are touched by it. It is a gift of God generated in the interactive life.

The second is the recognition of the significance of community as the supporting context of all personal life on which all men depend and in which and for which they were created by God. Some theologians would call this the principle of justice. We believe this is a misleading abstraction and prefer to point to the describable reality of the human community of persons as having an inevitable claim upon our lives. It is the relational network of intersupporting life in which no one can be excluded or rejected from its benefits and opportunities without damage to and constriction of all of the "selves" involved.

One of the primary motifs of the Reformed Ethic has been termed "the doctrine of limitation" and rests upon the Christian recognition of the sinfulness or untrustworthiness of all men. This means that no human being escapes being influenced by the value systems and the prevailing expectancies of the organizations in which he works. It is expecting too much of men to depend on personal inner character to produce responsibility in organizations that do not support it or even reject it. We have called this extra personal factor the structure of responsibility in the institutional patterns themselves. When a corporation expects price-fixing, either explicitly or implicitly, of its department heads and then blames them for not being honest when exposed, this additional requirement for responsibility is clearly demonstrated.

Therefore, Christian participants, in forming organizational policy, will work with others for codes of ethical practices in their organization to surround employees with a formal expectancy and pattern of fairness and responsibility. This is not inconsistent with our vigorous rejection of the view that Christian faith presents a moralistic code of absolutes. A business code of ethical practices in a plant or in an industry creates a spirit and an approval system that honors fairness and responsibility. It must be open to revision and be based on respect for persons and responsibility for the public good.

The same doctrine of limitation requires the Christian in economic life to accept the legitimacy of countervailing groups and to give serious consideration to their claims and interests. This is the recognition of the need of an "over-againstness" to offset our human overclaims and self-deceptions. In politics, this is the principle of "the loyal opposition," and in economic thinking it is the recognition of the need to have strong competitors. The Christian carries this even farther and holds that the claims of the opposition are more than economically competitive; they are also moral and religious counter-claims against our irresponsibilities. Moreover it is the Christian conviction that God is acting upon us through the claims of opponents in all decisions.

Under the same view, the Christian must recognize the inadequacy of voluntary organizations to provide a balanced pressure system as a context of responsibility and will welcome government as the representative of the whole community as a participant. Large numbers of people are not represented in the competition of organizations and sink into impoverishment and powerlessness unless their interests are pressed by government.

Regulatory laws to set fair standards and protect all citizens from fraud, misrepresentation, discrimination in employment, and dangerous products will be welcomed by those who believe in the doctrine of limitation. Definitions of fair standards are not moral absolutes but provisional agreements open to revision.

Between the tensions of large private centers of economic power and government power, all interdependent in a basic sense, lies the best hope of creating a responsible community and a responsible economic life in which there is the fairest possible distribution of economic opportunity. Under this kind of balance, the tyrannies of communist dictatorship and the disorders and inequities of unaccountable power seem most likely to be avoided.

DECIDING FOR THE FUTURE

There is a kind of decision-making that increasingly dominates the organizational world that some existentialist views of Christian responsibility tend to neglect. This is the policy or planning decision. Corporations and large organizations do not make their most important decisions moment by moment on a hand-to-mouth basis. They set goals and engage in long-range planning. In a limited way, they attempt to guide the processes toward hoped-for ends. This is a kind of limited or provisional idealism.

The Christian, as a responsible participant in the processes of decision in economic life, must work as such a provisional idealist toward patterns of greater accountability, toward a more inclusive community, and toward the raising of the opportunities of the impoverished. However, he must also be a faithful revisionist, never absolutizing these working goals, as he finds both new insight and new opportunities for responsible decision as God opens the way.

THE CHURCH AS CONTEXT
OF CHRISTIAN DECISION-MAKING

The Christian church is the beachhead of Christ in the world. One Christian alone is no Christian amid the pressures of a secular society. It is in the church among the people of God, in spite of all its dereliction and accommodation to the petty moralism and loyalties of the world, that he celebrates the sovereignty of the one God in whom all exist and renews his supreme covenant and identity in Christ.

While the Christian church has no sharp moral absolutes to guide its members in the hard arena of economic decision-making, it does provide something infinitely more significant. This is the fellowship of the Spirit in which is generated mutual self-criticism and support in confronting all decisions to be made. Too often the church has misrepresented itself to the outsiders in the world and consequently been misunderstood. Instead of divine laws for economic guidance, it offers the provisional judgments of Christians, consisting of their very human sense of present responsibility. Under this modest claim, it is the obligation of Christians and the church to make corporate judgments about the great issues of economic responsibility as the Holy Spirit leads them and corrects them.

Questions for Study and Discussion

Chapter I. The Tragic Separation

1. Why cannot economic life be separated and studied in its own enclosed system?

2. What is the tragic separation between the spiritual and the material and how does it confuse Christian responsibility in economic life?

3. Do you believe that American economic thinking is system-oriented and its ethical thinking is person-oriented? How has this contributed to the "tragic separation"?

4. In what way does occupational life have central spiritual significance?

Chapter II. The Big Change

1. What is a social crisis?

2. In what ways has the "big change" created a crisis in economic life?

3. Describe the organizational revolution and indicate how it has changed the way most Americans make a living.

Chapter III. The Embattled Protestant Ethic

1. What did Whyte mean by the Protestant Ethic?

2. Contrast the chief differences between the so-called Protestant Ethic and what we have called the Reformed Ethic.

3. In what sense is Protestantism antimoralistic?

89

Chapter IV. The Reformed Ethic of the American Puritans

1. What were the three guiding doctrines of the early Puritans?

2. Why did the transfer of God's work almost wholly to inner consciousness have fateful consequences for economic life?

3. What effect did social Darwinism have on the secularization of the Protestant Ethic?

Chapter V. The Business Ethic and the Reformed Ethic

1. What were the principal emphases of the business creed, as listed?

2. Why is uncritical optimism contrary to the basic Protestant understanding of man?

3. Do you believe we have had a decline in competition? In what way? Illustrate!

Chapter VI. Convergence in Decision

1. In what ways do faith and economic responsibility converge in the decision?

2. Is it ethical to charge an exorbitant price for something that is desperately needed by a customer and otherwise unavailable?

3. In what ways should the church intervene in or try to influence economic life?